PRAISE FOR
IN DEFENSE OF KINDNESS

"A simple yet staggering work that examines a precious and rare commodity in this present world, *In Defense of Kindness* made me think hard about my own actions and attitudes in ways that were admittedly uncomfortable. Woven through with personal anecdotes, observations, and memories, it's not a 'self-help' work but a companion for self-awareness. Bruce's book is deeply needed, and an essential jumping-off point for the conversations that might actually heal our vast and jagged national divides."

—JEFF YANG, CNN columnist,
cohost of the podcast *They Call Us Bruce*,
and coauthor of the forthcoming book
*Rise: A Pop History of Asian America,
from the Nineties to Now*

"*In Defense of Kindness* brings a much-needed message in a world filled with violence, intolerance, poverty, and racism. Organized into chapters that weave personal reflection and anecdotes with important topics like conflict, forgiveness, direct action, and institutional change, the book passionately and humorously argues that society suffers from a lack of kindness. Reyes-Chow does not indulge in nostalgic views of 'gentler times,' nor a definition of kindness that is simply about being nice to those you agree with (or even vehemently

D0111959

disagree with), but treats kindness as a serious balm for our personal and political lives and the social justice struggles of our day."

—LIZ THEOHARIS, director of the
Kairos Center for Religions, Rights, and Social Justice
at Union Theological Seminary and cochair of the
Poor People's Campaign: A National Call for Moral Revival

"I love this book. I needed this book. And part of the reason I love it so much is I can tell Bruce wrote it because he needed it, too. Instead of feeling preached at or judged because I don't really feel like being kind these days, Bruce made me chuckle and made me feel like it's okay that I feel that way, and helped remind me that maybe kindness is part of how we fight injustice. (Oh, spoiler: kindness and justice are complementary, not antithetical. That was good news also.)"

—SANDHYA RANI JHA, founder and director
of the Oakland Peace Center and author of
Liberating Love: 365 Love Notes from God

"Like a sinkhole, toxic masculinity has opened a chasm that threatens to swallow our world whole. Practiced by men and women; conservative and liberal; woke wannabes and white nationalists alike, the devaluation of kindness promises power but delivers destruction. With wit and heft, Bruce Reyes-Chow's *In Defense of Kindness* lights a candle and guides us out of the grift. Reyes-Chow points the way to what our truest selves long for—to be well."

—LISA SHARON HARPER, author of
*The Very Good Gospel:
How Everything Wrong Can Be Made Right*

"In an age where kindness is needed more than ever before, Bruce Reyes-Chow has given us a beautiful book weaving us back into community with each other. He reminds us of our deepest calling: to be kind...to ourselves, one another, and our world. The kindness that he outlines is not soft, wimpy, or weak. Kindness, according to Reyes-Chow, has passion, backbone, strength, vulnerability, courage, and relentless grace. Kindness is the fertile soil of our deepest transformation. I highly recommend this book for anyone wishing to make this world more kind, just, and generous."

—CAMERON TRIMBLE, executive director of Convergence

"In this essential read, Bruce Reyes-Chow translates his life of living and teaching kindness into this powerful guide that reminds us of the importance of kindness in our daily lives. In a time of constant change, there could hardly be a more important lesson than this."

—ROHIT BHARGAVA, bestselling author of
Non-Obvious Megatrends

"Through humor, personal story, and gentle guidance, Reyes-Chow wins us over in *In Defense of Kindness*, bringing us out of our cynicism and doubts to believe and choose a life of kindness. With concrete suggestions for everyday situations, from family to street protest, the book illuminates that a brave kindness wields the power to transform."

—DEBORAH LEE, executive director of
Interfaith Movement for Human Integrity

"At a time of profound discontent across the country, Bruce Reyes-Chow challenges readers to reimage the power of kindness as a way of being in the world. Using personal stories and self-deprecating humor, the author demonstrates how kindness is a powerful resource for personal growth and radical social change."

—SUSAN E. YOUNG, director of
religious and spiritual life at Occidental College

"Reyes-Chow not only offers excellent insights in this book, delivered with his usual cheeky wit and disarming authenticity, but he also assigns practical homework at the end of each section to help us bridge the gap between pondering kindness and actually working out our kindness muscles. Highly recommended."

—DAVID LAMOTTE, songwriter and author of
Worldchanging 101: Challenging the Myth of Powerlessness

"A book on kindness seems like swimming upstream right now—but it's good medicine for what ails us. I appreciated the encouragement and the thoughtful reflection about what kindness might look like in different arenas of life. All with an enjoyable dose of playful humor. Well worth the brief time it takes to read it."

—ALEXIA SALVATIERRA, assistant professor of
integral mission and global transformation at
Fuller Theological Seminary and coauthor of *Faith-Rooted
Organizing: Mobilizing the Church in Service to the World*

"Choosing kindness is a difficult yet life-giving decision. Thankfully, Bruce Reyes-Chow has written a helpful guide for all of us on this journey. He invites us to defend the human dignity of all people and orient our lives accordingly. This book will make a difference in the lives of its readers and our communal life as well."

—GUTHRIE GRAVES-FITZSIMMONS, author of
Just Faith: Reclaiming Progressive Christianity

"In an age when bullying behavior is so pervasive—whether in playgrounds, pulpits, or from political leaders—Bruce Reyes-Chow calls for a return to kindness. With self-reflective honesty and vulnerability, he shows us what a life of kindness entails. From the personal sphere to the public square, *In Defense of Kindness* challenges us to look at relationships through the lens of dignity and respect and engage in behaviors that center kindness as a radical act that honors the humanity of us all."

—**BISHOP KAREN OLIVETO**, Mountain Sky Conference, the United Methodist Church

"We strive to teach our children to be kind, but how do we navigate a world that has increasingly lost its faith in the value of kindness? *In Defense of Kindness* is a thoughtful, introspective, and timely exploration of what it means to actively choose kindness as a political and personal principle—a much-needed salve as we emerge out of the darkness of the last four years and take a healing step toward a brighter (and hopefully, kinder) future."

—**JENN FANG**, founder of Reappropriate

"Bruce beautifully brings into focus a much-needed cause for each of us to champion. An antidote for our current malaise. Choosing kindness can be quite complex. This is a simple yet heroic book, much like kindness can be a simple yet heroic act in itself."

—**DARREN A. KAWAII**, educator/activist

"In this timely book, Bruce Reyes-Chow shows just how much kindness affects our whole way of being and offers practical and relevant ways for healing our world's divisions and conflicts, as well as deeply personal relationships. What an important, authentic, and inspiring reminder to appreciate kindness and dare to incorporate it once again into our daily living!"

—JANIE SPAHR, PC(USA) minister and LGBTQ+ activist

"In an age in which meanness is not only encouraged but celebrated, Bruce Reyes-Chow provides a healing balm. With humor, honesty, wisdom, and practical advice, *In Defense of Kindness* will help you discover the hopeful, courageous, and generous spirit that waits within every human heart."

—MARK YACONELLI, author of *The Gift of Hard Things*

"This book gives me hope. Bruce Reyes-Chow has crafted a guidebook for expanding and integrating the practice of kindness into everyday leadership for people of diverse backgrounds for all communities. Each chapter introduces a personal story and meaningful scenario with thoughtful prompts for deeper introspection and immediate action. *In Defense of Kindness* is a treat, a treatise, and a necessary call to action. This book is required reading for those aspiring to or practicing intentional leadership in our times."

—JULIUS PARAS, curator at Filamthropy

"Bruce is the companion and teacher I need to be a more loving spouse, parent, friend, and leader. His in-depth exploration of kindness is a tool we need to become the community we are called to be."

—ABBY KING-KAISER, director of the
Dorothy Day Center for Faith and Justice at Xavier University

"Wielding kindness is a powerful, effective, impactful tool in your arsenal, far too important to be a bumper sticker for random acts. Bruce Reyes-Chow has considered the implications of intentional kindness and created a comprehensive how-to guide for recognizing the opportunity and benefits of factoring in kindness in our lives—making critical decisions, building a positive foundation, building team cohesiveness, and keeping communities connected. *In Defense of Kindness* amplifies our mission of supporting leadership through sport, and I can't recommend it highly enough to our players, coaches, and families."

—SCOTTYKOBER, executive director of
San Francisco Youth Soccer

"In a time when polarization and division seem to define our society, we need an honest talk about what kindness means. Through family stories, personal experiences, humor, and wisdom gathered over the years, Bruce takes the superficial understanding of kindness, turns it on its side, expands it, and shows us tangible ways to make it a way of life."

—JEREMY WILHELMI, chaplain of University of the Ozarks

IN DEFENSE OF KINDNESS

IN DEFENSE OF
KINDNESS

Why It Matters,
How It Changes Our Lives, and
How It Can Save the World

Bruce Reyes-Chow

CHALICE
PRESS

Saint Louis, Missouri

An imprint of Christian Board of Publication

Proofreaders: Kristen Hall-Geisler, Jenn Zaczek, and Sarah Currin
Interior book designer: Olivia Croom Hammerman
www.indigoediting.com

ChalicePress.com

Print: 9780827216761
EPUB: 9780827216778
EPDF: 9780827216785

Printed in the United States of America

There are three ways to ultimate success:
The first way is to be kind.
The second way is to be kind.
The third way is to be kind.
—Rev. Fred Rogers

#InDefenseOfKindness

CONTENTS

PREFACE

Ugh, That Mr. Rogers!

*I hope you're proud of yourself for the times you've said "yes,"
when all it meant was extra work for you and was seemingly
helpful only to somebody else.*
—Rev. Dr. Mr. Fred Rogers

SITTING IN THE movie theater one summer night in 2018, I realized that Mr. Rogers was not only a good storyteller, a carer of children's spirits, and a bringer of joy. Mr. Rogers was also a prophetic pain.

My family and I were watching the documentary *Won't You Be My Neighbor?*, which told the story of this Presbyterian pastor and person of faith as he struggled to convince the world and communicate to children that love, compassion, and kindness are powerful tools for healing, peace, and justice. In 2018, politicians, professional commentators, and armchair pundits seemed to be doing anything but extending kindness toward one another and anyone who disagreed with them. As I sat in the theater that night, I became acutely aware of two things about myself. First, in becoming increasingly subsumed by the constant barrage of hate, I was losing my ability and desire to regard my deepest political, theological, and ideological "enemies" as divinely created, complex, and beloved human beings. Second, my long-held belief that treating human beings as human beings is a transformative, healing, and needed witness in the world was fading fast.

About a year prior to this cinematic reintroduction to the message of Mr. Rogers, I had walked away from this kindness book project. Affected by the dumpster fire of our political climate, I was becoming cynical and was no longer claiming—let alone practicing—kindness as my way of being in the world. I found myself increasingly unable to extend kindness to some people. Frankly, I had become caught up in my own warped understanding of what it means to be kind rather than to be nice. I had become lazy in my calling to be in the world differently, especially in times of great human conflict. I was still talking a big game, but practically speaking, I had in many ways given up.

Like so many other people, I stress eating like a beast and packing on the poundage, and I could feel my accustomed empathy fading and my hopeful spirit calcifying.

And then along came Mr. Rogers and his kindness nonsense.

That night in the theater, as Mr. Rogers's story unfolded, I was jarred into the realization that a lack of empathy had taken root in me in ways much deeper and more dangerous than I had recognized. Mr. Rogers's righteous indignation, his love of children, and his deep faith reminded me that to love and to be kind are immensely powerful responses to injustice and pain in the world. They are the right way to be.

I could not, would not, allow my commitment to kindness to be a casualty of the disheartening and demeaning political war raging around me.

It was as if I heard Mr. Rogers talking directly to me: "Bruce, you know that kindness is powerful. You have always known that. So get over yourself, get yourself in gear, and get back to it."

Oh, how I do love to imagine being dressed down by the genteel cardigan prince!

After a few more moments of dialogue between the Fred in my head and me, I leaned over to my wife and said with some combination of resignation and excitement, "I think I have to finish my book on kindness."

The very next day, I received an email from Brad, publisher at Chalice Press, checking in to see how I was feeling about returning to The Kindness Project. After a moment of thinking, *Whoa, that's weird*, I said, "Yes. I'm in."

So here I am, pleading my case for kindness.

AN INTRODUCTION

I LOVE, LOVE, love it when people tell me what a stellar dad I am, or when they say my kids are lucky to have me as a parent. Suddenly, written on the sunny, blue-sky canvas of my mind in bold, rainbow-smoke writing, I see, "Yeah, I *am* a great dad."

(Cue William Shatner with my pageant sash, flowers, and crown.)

Soon after my confetti-strewn metaphorical walk down the runway to accept my accolades and tiara, I come to the sobering realization that today the bar to achieve "good dad" status is set pretty low. In a society that considers it normal for a mom to manage a successful career and master household management all while looking perfect and put together, it's not all that hard to be a "great dad." Heck, even when I'm unshowered and in ripped jeans and a dirty T-shirt, if people see me doing a couple of school pickups and drop-offs or shopping for family sustenance at the local gas station food mart, I'm the star.

Seriously, sometimes it must suck to be a mom these days.

Sidebar: Honey, I love and appreciate you :-)

The same society that expects so much of moms expects so little from dads. We have made being a good dad—let alone a *great* dad—the exception and have failed to demand and hold people accountable for being merely a decent parent. And we dads, because we benefit from this situation, have unwittingly reinforced this narrative that has allowed us to shirk our responsibilities, feed our tender egos, and reimagine what it is to be a good parent today. We buy into the low expectations. So we either stop trying, we fall into a posture of exerting minimal effort, or we come to expect the accolades as the norm.

We get lazy and start to believe the hype.

Repeat sidebar: Honey, I love and appreciate you :-)

Now if this social conundrum were just about the dads or only about my individual need to expand my understanding of my actions as a parent, we could simply continue to slough off some dads with an, "Oh, that's just the way David is. He's just a mediocre stepdad" (more on David, my mediocre stepdad, later) and be on our way. Who cares how other dads act as long as people still think *I'm* a great dad, right? The thing is, while it's ego-feeding for me, this is a pretty shortsighted approach to the great parenting endeavor. This parenting thing is not just about us—dads, moms, nonbinary coparents, or anyone else who participates in the raising of children today (which, BTW, I believe is everyone). Every time we buy into this narrative that being a committed, caring, and loving dad is the exception, we pass on to future generations this flawed and destructive narrative. We will continue to expect women to live up to unreasonable and oppressive expectations of motherhood, and we dads will continue to be seduced by the idea that the world should be grateful that we are doing the bare minimum and that the bare minimum is all we need to do.

So what does all this have to do with kindness?

Just as buying into the low-bar approach is no way to go about being a parent, we must do our best to avoid setting the bar just as low when it comes to kindness.

Alas, I fear it is too late. We have lowered the kindness bar, and we have become lazy. Given the increased visibility (through social media in particular) of expressions of violence, xenophobia, racism, misogyny, ableism, and more, it is no longer all that hard to be seen as a kind person because the bar has been lowered to the point that simply *not* being violent, xenophobic, racist, misogynistic, or ableist is all one has to do in order to be kind. Dehumanization and dismissiveness have become the norm to such an extent that when we notice the infrequent whisper of a kind act or word or response, we are shocked into whipping our out smartphone, recording it, and sharing it with the world. Nowadays even the simplest acts of kindness are newsworthy and become viral sensations: being patient with an older person in the checkout line, providing help to someone who is of another race, taking time to assist someone with a physical disability, and yes, being a dad who shows emotion and compassion to their child.

Kindness can and should be celebrated. Still, I fear that we are now at a point when highlighting kindness in such ways not only makes being kind seem like a herculean, heroic, and exhausting gesture, but it also diverts our attention away from addressing the root causes of oppression and injustice that have put so many people in positions where simple acts of kindness are needed in order to alleviate suffering.

Take, for instance, my general examples above:

Example #1: Yes, celebrate when people respect our elders. But let's also ask the question, "Why do we, in the United States, have such an anti-elderly culture?"

Example #2: Yes, celebrate when folks cross racial divides. But let's also ask the questions, "In what ways has the United States been built upon the foundation of slavery and racism? What steps can I take to recognize and dismantle that foundation?"

Example #3: Yes, celebrate when people go out of their way to help someone. But let's also ask the question, "Why do we still see disabled persons as less than?"

Example #4: Yes, it's great that dads are in touch with the emotional needs of their children. But let's also ask the question, "Why do men get parades for doing what should be assumed (and is assumed about women)?"

I am not against celebrating acts of kindness. But I am perplexed by the attitude that being kind is beyond most mortals' reach, so why bother? No—every single person has the capacity to be kind. Being kind is not a superpower; it is a way of being that we must and can choose every day.

Am I overstating the lack of kindness? Try the following:

- Name the last two or three acts of kindness that you witnessed, read about, or watched on social media, television, or in person.
- Name the last two or three hurtful, hateful, or dehumanizing acts that you witnessed, read about, or watched on social media, television, or in person.

How long did you have to think? I bet that examples of the latter came to you far faster than the former. Has it always been that way? Why accept that as a good reason? If people are always going to kill other people, should we no longer try to stop the killing? Even if there will always be those who become addicted to drugs or alcohol, does that mean we should stop educating people about the dangers of addiction and substance abuse? If there will always be people in the world who find fulfillment in their lives by belittling, bullying, and dismissing others, does that mean we should stop trying to lift people up, stop fostering self-worth in our children, and stop creating a more hospitable and welcoming society? It is precisely because so much that is not kind has become normalized that we must be that much more kind in response.

The positive pressures to be kind simply are not as prevalent as they once were. From small gestures, like offering a seat on the bus to an elderly rider, to how we engage in political discourse on Twitter, our ways of being have changed—and not for the better.

Being kind is a challenging endeavor. It's a way of being in the world that we have to practice. But when we model mediocre kindness, we give in to a world guided by intolerance, indifference, and hostility.

This must change, and I choose to believe we can and must make it happen.

Before you start to believe that the world is entirely devoid of goodness and joy, let me say that I do believe that many acts of kindness occur every day. We do not always notice them, but from the subtle to the stupendous, I do know that kindness exists. I will talk about more kindness in a viral sense, but here are just a few subtle moments of kindness that come to mind from my life:

- The barista who on occasion just waves me off when I try to pay for my "Iced Greater Haze, sweet and creamy, Stevia, and cinnamon and nutmeg in the filter" coffee (don't judge—it's joy in a cup)

- A friend who drove to the airport at 3:00 a.m. to pick up our sixteen-year-old daughter who was stranded after her flight was canceled
- Our new neighbor knocking on our door wondering if that "white dog wandering down the street" belongs to us

These are not earth-shattering acts of kindness. They indict change in my life by the everyday simplicity with which they are offered. Kindness as a lens through which we live our lives does not need reinvention; instead, to see the world of the future as building on the actions of kindness of past generations, we must reinforce, recapture, and reimagine the healing, power, and liberation that kindness brings the world.

I will dive deeper into what kindness is before long, but I know that some of you are already thinking, "Kindness is all well and good, but being 'nice' simply won't cut it." I understand. But even or particularly in the most conflicted of situations, is there really no use for kindness, graciousness, and decency? Are we really willing to feed the idea that the normative way of interacting today is *not* to be nice, let alone kind?

Kindness challenges those people who are fed by being hurtful and who find worth by tearing others down. This is not the posture that I intend to live in the world. The posture of tearing another down believes that the only way to "win" is to gain power over others, to make the other feel less than, and to get to a point of submission and victory. That is a sure way to bankrupt our souls.

Kindness has power if we not only believe in it but also live it into being. I choose to practice standing on the side of kindness. It may be a struggle, but to quote the fictional character Jimmy Dugan talking to a discouraged baseball player in Penny Marshall's movie classic *A League of Their Own*, "It's supposed to be hard. If it wasn't hard, everyone would do it. The hard is what makes it great." Yes, to be kind can be hard. If it were easy, everyone would do it. But seeing Mr. Rogers again reminded me that I want to rediscover the power of kindness, to witness how it can move us through even the most difficult of situations, to be an agent of kindness myself.

In Defense of Kindness is for two sorts of people. If you are someone who already strives for kindness every day, I hope the company of this book and its stories will encourage and energize you to continue knowing you are not alone in this endeavor. If, on the other hand, you understand the concept of kindness intellectually but are still unsure whether being kind is worth the time and energy, this book will remind you—and I hope convince you through theory and practice—that by embracing kindness in new, contextual, and intentional ways, you will make the world a healthier, more liberating, and kinder place.

If, on the other hand, you are a card-carrying, hard-core anti-kindness activist, this book will only give you nightmares—nightmares of hope, optimism, and rainbow-farting unicorns, but nightmares nonetheless.

You have been warned.

I choose to believe that being kind is the most powerful way to invite positive change into the world. But I know that, even on my best days, being kind is more aspirational than actual, and I cannot do this kindness thing all by myself. Having you for company will make me more likely to be kind. Won't you join me on this journey?

For Reflection:
More than anything else, what prevents you
from being kind?
Where is kindness most needed?

Try This:
Make a list of three people you know who exemplify
a life of kindness.
Send them a note to thank them for being kind.

Kindness Defined

A PUPPY'S LOVE is so darn compelling that, if you saw your worst enemy—let's call him Patrick, the guy who bullied you all the way through high school by leaning on your locker so you couldn't open it and made you late to class—walking down the street, there would undoubtedly be some melting of the ice if, bouncing right by his side, was the cutest puppy you'd ever seen. Seriously, how could such an awful person like hypothetical Patrick have not only such a happy dog but also one that seems to think Patrick deserves the joy that this puppy exudes? Doesn't that puppy know what a jerk her owner is?

I'll tell you why that ice melted a little.

Dogs are kind.

And that particular dog probably does know what a jerk Patrick is, but she treats him the same way each and every day anyway.

Traitor.

Okay, I know that dogs are neither made of pure sunshine nor immune from the temptation of self-interest. I am also aware that dogs see humans as the ones who satisfy their need to eat, who open the door when they need to poop, and who pretty much pet them at the first glance of those big puppy eyes. So no, they are not actually "selfless." But I am going to continue to choose to believe that when I come home each day, my puppies, with every cell of their bodies, are thinking,

My human is home, my human is home! I love him, and he's the best human ever.

Kindness in its purest form is about simply responding to the interests of the person before you.

Other people's descriptions of kindness flesh it out some more:

> Kindness is…love and mercy. And love and mercy are challenging, messy, heartbreaking, and painful, and yet it is the only work that gives us breath and makes life worth living.
> —Andy Acton, @georgiapreacher

> Kindness is…giving others the benefit of the doubt, the most generous assumption until proven otherwise.
> —Cindy Wunder, @cascadiagrl

> Kindness is…being willing to place the importance of the relationship above the importance of being right.
> —Pepa Paniagua, @pepajean

> Kindness is…the gateway to love.
> —Audrey Garcia, @audrygarcia

Because we have all lived different lives and have experienced kindness as well as hatred in various ways, our expressions of kindness will be as diverse as the people with whom we live. Here's my working definition of what it means to be kind: *To be kind is to accept that each person is a created and complex human being—and to treat them as if you believe this to be true.* Such a definition of kindness challenges me to see and treat the other as complex, created, and worthy of dignity. That takes work. Imagine:

The Politician who stands against everything in which I believe. As distasteful and dangerous as their politics may be to me, if I am kind, I can begin by acknowledging that they too are probably carrying sadness and struggle borne of personal tragedy and loss. To be kind to The Politician means holding them accountable without denying their personal struggles and experiences.

The Saint who always seems to act justly. Surely even the Mr. Rogers types of the world succumb to the emotionality of injustice and wrongs in the world occasionally. To be kind to The Saint means allowing them to live and express the fullness of human emotion and not to expect them to be perfect all the time.

The Immigrant, the "other," who often bears the brunt of our blame for the faults of our part of the world. To be kind to The Immigrant means acknowledging and trying to understand the complexity of their experiences: their personhood, agency, struggles, hardships, opportunities, and joys.

The Celebrity who we think deserves our criticism for making a bad movie choice, committing an error during a crucial game, looking disheveled when they are out buying groceries, or dating (or not dating) a particular person. To be kind to The Celebrity means remembering that who the person is in public likely does not represent them fully and that they too carry life experiences, as the rest of us do.

The Ideologue, the person who sees themselves as the protector of a belief system or political position and does so intransigently. To be kind to The Ideologue means remembering that every person behind a screen has been formed by life experiences that may be much like our own and to practice restraint in our responses to them.

Examples abound of how we reduce one another—and ourselves—to one dimension, one characteristic. When we normalize such a way of interacting, we create relationships that lack substance or depth. Worse still, we create dangerous and oppressive systems and institutions that are built on narrow experiences of the other and false narratives about who people are or can become.

Kindness is not just the absence of being mean or hateful. Being kind entails actively resisting actions, ideas, and institutions that rob others of dignity.

The rest of this book will help address the nuances of what I hope kindness looks like in the world, but because I am sure that you have been thinking, *Yeah, but what about…?* or *What exactly do you mean by…?* let me unpack my definition a little more fully.

To be kind is to accept that each person is a created and complex human being—and to treat them as if you believe this to be true.

To accept that each person—Kindness begins with being able to accept that each person is an individual human being. Yes, human to human, we are shaped and formed by culture and context. Some commonalities are shared, but taken in totality, no two people on this earth are exactly the same. Each person is unique.

Is a created and complex human being—Assuming that each person is a unique individual, kindness also demands that we acknowledge that each person has been formed by personal experiences, both good and bad, and that no one is as one-dimensional as we would like to believe them to be. Each person experiences jubilation, disappointment, hopelessness, despair, and so on—you, me, them. Words like *joy, laughter, grief,* and *confusion* conjure up memories and images of when we have experienced these reactions. In turn, each of us is then shaped by these memories, lessons, and perspectives. Knowing that, kindness demands we acknowledge that even our worst enemy, who is full of bluster and bravado, has known the highs and lows of life, just as we all have.

And to treat them—Few of us have the resources or yearning to drop off the social grid and remove ourselves from any and all human interaction. So at some point, each of us has to interact with another human. Every interaction either builds up or tears down. Thus every action and interaction, no matter how small it might be, has an impact on the other person or persons involved. Whether you believe that or not, to err on the side of "how I treat others matters more than I could imagine" is not a bad way to go. For this reason, to be kind is to remember that each interaction we have with another person, be it face-to-face conversations or social network commentary, matters and makes a difference.

As if you believe this to be true—In an ideal world, when we "accept" something, the natural progression is that this acceptance manifests itself in behaviors that reflect that acceptance. Of course this can be good or bad depending on the behavior, but I choose to believe that if someone truly sees me as a complex human being with a life story that has multiple places of connection, we can passionately disagree with one another—even be enraged with one another—without falling into the trap of stripping away one another's humanity.

Okay, by now you have begun to develop some questions about kindness and how I have presented it thus far. If my ideas seem too simple or Pollyannaish for you, rest assured that my understanding of kindness is not a call to a utopian world of niceties, but a nuanced way for us to move forward together, as diverse and divided as we are, with some strings of common understanding and shared empathy that will positively affect how we live together as a society and community.

I hope that you are open to seeing the abundant kindness that I believe you already possess and that you will find some ways in the next few chapters to express that kindness with bold, almost reckless abandon.

Let's do this!

For Reflection:

How would you define kindness?

Share a few aspects of yourself that are often overlooked or misunderstood.

Try This:

To whom do you find it most difficult to be kind?

Kindness Debunked

WE AFFECTIONATELY CALL our middle daughter, Abby, "Junkyard Piglet." She's so cute, petite, unassuming, and quiet that one could easily mistake her for being docile, weak, and yes, nice. There are many people in her life who will let you know that you should make this assessment at your own risk: siblings, classmates, soccer opponents, teachers, and yep, her parentals. While she is kind and empathetic, and she does try to see the best in others, she is not "nice" in a weak way. One should not let one's guard down or try to take advantage of her hoping that she will not respond with strength, will, or a well-timed reminder that Junkyard Piglet is in the house!

One of my favorite pins says, "Do not mistake my kindness for weakness." It encapsulates one of the misconceptions of kindness—that to be kind is to be weak.

Let's get one thing straight: being kind is not about being nice. While being nice is not a bad thing in general, often being nice is an outward action that is more about not rocking the boat than about acknowledging the human dignity of others. Being nice is often about avoiding conflict, letting inappropriate actions slide, or bottling up words and actions that ought to be spoken and enacted to prevent creating an uncomfortable scene. At its worst, being nice reinforces actions and attitudes that strip away human dignity. So if that's what you are doing, then yes, I say stop doing that.

Don't confuse conflict-avoiding niceness with dignity-seeking kindness, for when you do, the kindness-hater will be right: you are just being nice.

A few other critiques that you may receive:

"You just want to get along." Since when did getting along become bad? Sure, if getting along comes at the expense of the dignity of others, then no, don't do that. But as a general rule, getting along, creating community, and seeking the common good can all be manifestations of being kind, welcoming people to the table, and seeing the humanity in one another.

"If you're making someone mad, you're doing something right." Conversely, this can be read as, "If you're not annoying people, then you're not doing something right." Sure, people will get mad because you are filled with righteous indignation and are standing up against injustice in the world. The danger is to start with getting people mad as the ultimate goal. Not only does this approach create strategic roadblocks to change, but it also cheapens the impact of prophetic voices that do not seek to make people mad, only to speak truth to power in ways that the world may not hear.

"You are being naive." Do not let the cynics win! There will always be times when we are feeling overwhelmed by the news of global destruction and we become frustrated by the political tweetstorms, and we may then think that noticing human complexities seems useless. Own the feelings. They are yours, and you would not

be human if you didn't sometimes feel as if the battle will never be won. But here is the thing: giving up and deciding that being kind to other humans beings is just not worth the time and energy is precisely what the ugly of the world want us to do. When we stop seeing the goodness around us and decide that a commitment to kindness is no longer worth it, we add to the pain that has created our feelings of being overwhelmed in the first place. To give in to this belief is a bankrupt and soul-sucking decision. Please do not give in to it. By committing yourself to a life of kindness, you are not being naive about the impact of your actions; you are being courageous and bold. You believe that your actions and attitudes can make a difference.

A word about "Bless your heart." I am not from the South, but from what my friends tell me, there is always a little passive-aggressive judgment present when someone says, "Bless your heart." I have heard people say it about other people with a tone of affection and care. But if it were really a good term, wouldn't people say it more often to people's faces? Whenever I see it being spoken directly to someone, it is *clearly* a passive-aggressive way of noting something that is foolish. It's like launching a veiled criticism at someone, and before the recipient can metaphorically punch the launcher in their metaphorical throat, the launcher quickly adds the disclaimer, "I'm just saying." Maybe that is the northern equivalent to "Bless your heart"? Well, no matter where you are from, if you choose kindness, you are bound to get looks or words with these sentiments behind them. I respond in two ways: ignore it or ask with as much genuineness as possible, "Why, thank you, but what do you mean by that?" or "Clearly you are not 'just saying.' So what *are* you saying?" By responding, not only are you not letting bad behavior pass and possibly making the person think more reflectively, but you may also be saving the next person from such treatment. And if you are now thinking to yourself, *Well, bless your heart, Bruce*, know that I am ignoring you.

If you are still on board the kindness train, at every stop someone is going to find a reason why the lens through which you view life is the wrong one. While it may be tempting to take on the naysayer right then with some passive-aggressive social media posting—a temporarily satisfying but lazy response, not that I have *ever* done such a thing—resist the urge and choose to confront the culture of kindness hating. Defend kindness by choosing each and every day to commit to this way of being.

Rest assured, the kindness-hating horde is lurking around every corner, just waiting for you to preach your kindness nonsense, so when you do find yourself starting to wonder if you are just being nice, or naive, or, or, or...reframe the conversation and re-energize your spirit by remembering this:

They say, "Kindness is weakness." I say, "Kindness is strength."

They say, "Kindness is naivete." I say, "Kindness is courage."

They say, "Kindness is superficial." I say, "Kindness has depth."

They say, "Kindness is passive." I say, "Kindness is active."

They say, "Kindness is complicity." I say, "Kindness is justice."

They say, "Kindness is abdication." I say, "Kindness is confrontation."

They say, "Kindness is abstract." I say, "Kindness is personal."

They say, "Kindness is distraction." I say, "Kindness is commitment."

They say, "Kindness is dumb." I say, "I know you are, but what am I?"*

They say, "Kindness is apathy." I say, "Kindness is engagement."

They say, "Kindness is disingenuous." I say, "Kindness is vulnerability."

They say, "Kindness is futile." I say, "Kindness is transformational."

---

*Just seeing if you're paying attention :-)

They say, "Kindness is convenient." I say, "Kindness is a lifestyle."

They say, "Kindness is a waste of time." I say, "Kindness is an abundance of hope."

They say, "Kindness is impossible." I say, "Kindness is imperative."

They say, "Kindness is dead." I say, "Kindness is life."

You will surely have moments in which you doubt the kindness way of life, but if you are still reading, one of two things is happening: either this is required reading for your class and you now wish you had registered for Zumba for Physics Majors, or there is a part of you that knows that kindness, in all its complexity, difficulty, and doubt, is worth living. There will always be voices of doubt screaming into your world, but I hope you will listen to that whisper from your soul that says kindness is the path for you. I hope that with each and every day with which you are gifted, from your first waking breath until your body, mind, and soul find rest at the end of your day, you will choose kindness.

For Reflection:
How would you define the difference between being kind and being nice or polite?
Share a time when you were accused of being too nice or polite when you were simply being kind.

Try This:
Survey the interactions of your last twenty-four hours and decide if you were being "kind" or just "nice."

Kindness as Commodity

My grandfather's name, Esteban de los Reyes, or Steven of the Kings, is a pretty cool name. Unfortunately, when he immigrated to the United States from the Philippines in 1928, the US government thought that it was just a bit too exotic and summarily changed it to Steve Reyes. Though this was the name he used as a teenager who found himself working in restaurants in Los Angeles, the name he used working the fields of the Central Valley of California picking tomatoes and strawberries, and the name he used getting to know the movers and shakers of Stockton, California, as a bartender at the local country club, to me my grandfather will always be that stylishly dressed young man worthy of the smooth name Esteban de los Reyes.

Grandpa Reyes was generous, playful, and always ready for a good cry that was either fueled by anger or born of joy. My mother tells me that when he got home from his shift at the bar, she and her siblings would hear his pocket jingling with coins. This meant that when he opened the door, coins came a-flying. It was like literal pennies falling from heaven as he tossed coins in the air for the kids to catch and keep.

He also felt deeply. Whether it was for a social injustice or the love of his family and kids, he had all the feels. Many a time he would just be sitting on the couch watching his grandchildren play, and he would start to weep with joy. Yep,

I'm crying as I write this. As we have learned, the crying is genetic—apologies to my children.

In the eyes of many, I am sure that all these traits put together made him appear too nice and, when it comes to his marriages, I would not disagree.

His first wife, my grandmother, was—how shall we say?— feisty, passionate, and determined. And truth be told, she took advantage of my grandfather. As she once wrote to my mother when talking about me as a child—I'll expand on this later—"When I met your dad, I told him I don't love him but I was willing to get married if I could have children. In the long run, I have been happy with him because of you kids."

If this were a movie, it would be some version of "The scrappy survivor meets the hopeless romantic."

The same personality and character traits that helped my grandmother survive being abandoned in Little Rock, Arkansas, then make it to California, get a job, and start a family also created situations in which she was not faithful to him. This forced him to make decisions that many would have seen as too nice and as allowing my grandmother to take advantage of his commitment to his children. There is a movie-deserving story here, but if you sense a bit of hesitance on my part, you would be correct. No one in the family knows many of the stories of their marriage and the decisions he made in response to her actions. While such stories would make poignant illustrations, I am choosing to be kind and let people pass down the stories when they are good and ready. Some of them are not my stories to share. They are intimate, painful, and raw, so I am choosing the kindness of discretion.

I did say "some stories" because I have no problem dishing on his other wives.

After my grandfather eventually divorced my grandmother, he remarried twice more, both times on trips to the Philippines to visit relatives. My grandfather craved and deserved companionship, so he married Tessie on his first visit to the Philippines. While a bit shocked, we were in some ways very happy for him. But the pattern of his wife taking advantage of his kindness was repeated. His second wife had some severe mental health issues that eventually led to us not being able to see him very much. When we pleaded with him to do something, his kindness was evident. Even though this was not an ideal marriage, he felt he was supposed to protect and care for her, and he did everything to maintain his marriage.

A few years into the marriage, Tessie died in a car accident, leaving my grandfather companionless again.

Some years later when Grandpa let us know that he was going to the Philippines for a visit, we all said, "Grandpa, *do not get married!*" Well, you can imagine how that went.

This time he married a much younger woman, one just a year older than my mother, and we knew from the start this was not going to be a good situation. The short version is that she blew through his savings, they lost his house, she moved him to San Diego, and often we could not even locate him for a visit. I cherish the few times that we were able to see him during those years, and I still get angry about what she did and what we were not able to do. She eventually let us know that he had died and that we needed to be "family" and pay her the respect due to our "grandmother."

That didn't happen.

Clearly my grandfather was kind to a fault. His kindness led him into painful situations, and I wish he had made different decisions. I would have loved for all of my children, my nieces, and his namesake, my nephew, Esteban, to have known this amazingly kind, generous, and loving human. They would have met a man who was empathetic with others' struggles, loyal to those in his community, and kind without expectation of reciprocation.

That kindness is not transactional is one of the greatest lessons I learned from him. While I wish that he had been more kind to himself, and while I would never want someone to be taken advantage of as he was, I err on the side of this sort of optimistic kindness every time. I do so out of a genuine belief that every person deserves to be seen as a human being and not because I expect the same treatment in return.

For if our commitment to kindness is contingent upon being repaid with the same posture and approach, we are in for a lifetime of frustration and a jaded future. If we make kindness contingent, then we have failed to examine the possible repercussions of the Golden Rule, "Do unto others as you would want others to do unto you." Two problems can come from not examining this rule. First, it is quite possible that the recipient of the treatment does not actually want to be treated in the same way that you do. If our social location and context become the norm, we treat people how we would want to be treated, assuming that they live in the same norm. A good example is how we greet one another. I tend to be a hugger, but not everyone likes to be hugged. The second potential problem with this saying is that there is an implicit understanding and expectation of reciprocation. If we take kindness and individual agency seriously, we will not read this rule as a transactional guarantee.

Nope, there are no guarantees that kindness will be reciprocated. We are kind not because of what we get out of the act, but because of what it says about how we understand the humanity of others and how we believe that humans should be treated.

Expressing kindness doesn't guarantee that we'll get kindness in return. But we hope that the more expressions and act of kindness there are, the more people will experience the world as benevolent. We hope that our acts and expressions of kindness will gradually result in a world that sees kindness not as a commodity to barter, but as a natural and normative way to treat everyone around us.

For Reflection:
What other human interactions are often considered as eliciting some kind of reciprocation?
Share a time when you were frustrated that your kindness was not reciprocated.

Try This:
The next time you say "Thank you," gauge how much you expect a response of "You're welcome." Reflect on your reaction.

Kindness as Competition

WHENEVER I HEAR or see the saying, "Kill them with kindness," I automatically think, *How about we don't kill anyone, with kindness or anything else?* I get it. The idea is that if we are kind to people, they'll have no choice but to bend to our will and change their perspective on life. Yes, that would be great. But when I had bullies in high school, or when people in my workplace were not behaving well, my refusal to reciprocate with bad behavior was not an act of kindness; it was a way of tapping into my survival and self-preservation skills. It would have been great if the bullies or ill-behaved colleagues had recognized their bad behavior and changed. But honestly all I cared about was not getting my butt kicked, physically or vocationally. If there was any kindness evident, it was me being kind to me.

Kindness used to gain something over another, as opposed to kindness being the normative way we should treat other humans regardless of advantage or position, is not kindness at all.

Sure, there are times when strategically approaching someone with kindness rather than with an adversarial or aggressive posture makes sense. But these are tactical decisions born out of necessity rather than being genuine and transformative gestures toward another human.

We must resist seeing kindness as a commodity or as a well-timed tactic or strategy that is likely to have an immediate and measurable outcome. Kindness is about recognizing the dignity of the human. It is not about reinforcing systems and cultures that sustain a false sense of meritocracy and victory over the other.

Stay with me on this.

Sometimes we try to out-kindness one another. Let's say we hear a story about how someone is being kind. We respond with another story about someone else being even kinder.

Like so many conversations these days, we have a hard time letting things stand on their own or letting the other person's story be enough. Sharing often becomes a game of one-upmanship.

When we establish rankings or a hierarchy of acts of kindness, we're on dangerous ground. Being kind is not about keeping score or about outdoing others. So the next time someone shares a story of kindness with you or you think of an act of kindness as a tactic, be careful. Try not to drift into the realm of competitive kindness, for in the kindness way of being, there are no ribbons or trophies, just the satisfaction that you have treated someone with dignity.

For Reflection:
When have you seen kindness being expressed
as a competition?
When have you seen kindness being used as a tactic?

Try This:
The next time someone shares a story, listen well,
and do not respond with your own story.

Kindness and Privilege

I ONCE HAD a conversation with someone during a protest and the taking over of a roadway in the San Francisco Bay Area. The protest occurred during the early stages of the #BlackLivesMatter movement. The social atmosphere in the United States was charged, to say the least. The conversation about this life-or-death reality boiled down to this response from a bystander: "If they did not inconvenience people so much, I would be much more supportive of their cause."

Kindness that merely placates those who are inflicting trauma, violence, or oppression may be a valid survival technique, but it centers the aggressor and allows them to dictate the future.

Kindness cannot be boiled down to specific, concrete, never-changing actions. How we express kindness depends on our own social context, experiences, culture, and privilege.

Likewise, it is not kind to tell someone who is expressing righteous and disruptive indignation to be "civil" or "appropriate." Historically, these kinds of admonishments have been code for "Stop creating discomfort," "Know your place," or "Shut up!" While I understand the desire to be more compassionate and to have more thoughtful engagement around disagreements, we must be careful that such a desire does not turn into a modern-day manifestation of "civilizing" those who do not fit into our understanding of normative behavior. Sometimes our norms oppress and marginalize others.

When acts of kindness and calls for civility are fueled by social, economic, and racial privilege, these acts are often more about doing just enough to keep the status quo and not about transformative change for those who are experiencing struggle. This call for civility is dangerous. It assumes that well-intentioned people or organizations will actively seek out their flaws and correct them without any prodding from others, whether insiders or outsiders. We know this to be untrue. Protest, disruption, and "uncivilized" behavior is precisely what compels individuals and organizations to change, sometimes willingly and with integrity and sometimes because market forces compel them to change or go out of business. The existence of any protections for and the civil rights of people of color, women, workers, LGBTQIA+ people, and countless others were all the result of people taking to the streets to protest injustice and unfair practices that needed to be named.

Not every expression offered in the face of injustice is justified or should be accepted simply because it is protest. Our first reaction to others pointing out injustices that might create discomfort in ourselves, our institutions, and our social status cannot be "We'll listen if you just stop yelling and talk calmly. Then you might have more impact." No doubt there will have been multiple attempts to work through the system, to use processes set up by the institution, and to be "appropriate," "respectful," "civil," and otherwise not make a scene. When those tactics do not result in change, it's appropriate to resort to public protest.

For many of us, being uncomfortable about public protest or what we perceive as aggressive expressions of frustration simply identifies our privilege and our ability to shield ourselves from the struggles that others are facing. May our call to civil discourse be more about listening to the genuine struggles of our human sisters, brothers, siblings, neighbors, and strangers than about protecting our own spaces of security. Most people do not engage in public protest or in expressing anger that may put at risk their life, work, or status. So when groups of people are pushed to their boiling point, the least helpful thing to do is to silence them.

Expressions of kindness in times of social change and public protest should focus on those who are seeking justice and liberation and *not* on the ones whose privileged worlds are being disrupted by the leveling of a social playing field or a correction in disparities of access, power, or authority. If someone is seeking civil rights through public protest or sharing their frustration in a way that causes us discomfort, rather than adopting a posture of defensiveness, a kinder response is for us to listen with empathy in order to seek true understanding. The second, third, and tenth acts of kindness are to discern how this knowledge and experience will affect future actions, all while keeping at the center of the conversation the voices of those whom the change will benefit. It takes control and wisdom to listen to justified expressions of frustrations. That too is an act of kindness.

For Reflection:
When have you participated in public protest, and what compelled you to do so?
When have you witnessed a protest and thought that it was "too much"? Why did you have that reaction?

Try This:
Scan your newsfeed for a protest happening somewhere in the world and note your initial reactions, then do some background research about the reason for the protest to see if your perspective changes.

Kindness and Conflict

BELOW IS A (slightly edited) letter that my grandmother wrote to my mother when I was just over a year old. At the time, my mother was struggling as a single mother and contemplating how to proceed with my custody. I share this not to discourage people from putting up their children for adoption but as my take on the way my grandmother stepped in to the situation. And while my grandmother was a force to be reckoned with, she was pretty insightful...especially the "he is a cute and wonderful baby" part.

In this letter from my grandmother, I am "Boo Boo" and Billy is my dad. My mother was living in Sacramento and working at the state legislature.

June 17, 1970

Dear Sarah,

I have been trying to get the courage to write you a short and big advice. Whether you take it or not, I don't really care.

The first time I hear[d] that you were giving up Boo Boo I really felt hurt, Daddy too, 'cause I never thought you were that hard at heart. I have experience being with a step-mother and it's not all roses. You can find a lot of husbands, but you are the only mother to your child.

You might think Boo Boo will be taken care of by Billy and his mother, but it's not the same like his own mother.

Boo Boo has been with Billy for two days now and by the time you get to see him, he won't even recognize you. Does this make you feel happy?

Before you got married you knew from the beginning that Bill had no job, but you were willing to stick it out with him.

Sarah, I didn't love your dad either but I had to stick it out because of you kids; but as a mother, I feel that I have failed all of you.

I divorced my first husband because we couldn't have kids. And when I met your dad, I told him I don't love him but I was willing to get married if I could have children. In the long run, I have been happy with him because of you kids.

Do think it out before you decide what to do with your life.

I am glad you have the courage to get away from Billy, but I hope not from Boo Boo. He is a cute and wonderful baby. I love him just like my own, but I really don't take care of him as a mother.

Don't mistake me, I do not want you to stay with Bill if you are not happy, but before you plan to get married again, I hope there will be no kids involved. So long for now, hope to hear from you soon.

Remember we will always love you, you will have a home any time you want to. Maybe when Senate closes for the summer.

Love, Mother

P.S. Make a reservation for a motel for me and Lina and Boo Boo if I can get him from Billy for June 26 and 27 (Friday and Saturday night) near Hughes Stadium by Broadway. See you then.

Billy is going to hire a lawyer and [file for] full custody of Boo Boo. His mother wants to adopt the baby.

In the end, my mother chose to keep me around. And for the most part—save a few times that I will reserve for my memoir—she has not regretted it. And now my siblings tease her that she is channeling Grandma, because there are times when it feels like that same crazy, loving, and stern lady has been reincarnated in the body of my mother. She has written letters to us in the same way, she has been lovingly firm when she has needed to, and most importantly, she has continued to believe we could make good choices in our lives even when we were not sure of that ourselves.

If you guessed that my grandmother was one of those people that you would probably love to watch move the world on her own terms but knew that you should not cross her, you would be correct. She was fiercely loving and even goofy at times, but not warm and fuzzy by any means. She knew what she knew and said what she said, no apologies. She also held grudges and didn't put up with foolishness.

My grandmother and my mother's relationship was complex because they are alike in many ways. It is hysterical and lovely to watch, but don't get on the wrong side of them! My favorite story is that on my mom's eighteenth birthday, she came home and there were moving boxes in her room. I am sure there was some fight in which that eighteen-year-old expressed her desire to move out and my grandmother called her bluff.

Don't threaten what you are not willing to back up. This is an excellent rule in life, work, and community—especially if you run into people like my mother or grandmother.

I share this letter because sometimes kindness means addressing important things, even knowing that it will exacerbate or create conflict. Kindness knows that if you do not act, the possible ramifications would be harmful to people involved. Kindness sometimes means risking relationships for the good of the people involved. If we genuinely value the dignity of each human being, we cannot stand by and allow people to make decisions that we believe are unwise, hurtful, or dangerous. Standing by without doing anything does not value their humanity; it just allows us to avoid conflict, discomfort, and the hard work of being in relationship.

One caveat: choosing to insert oneself into the situation of loved ones may not always be welcome or wise. Sometimes we can venture into places where we are trying to make people do what we want them to do rather than allowing them agency to make their own decisions. There are no hard and fast rules around this, for even when whatever you are suggesting may be the best thing to do, your loved one may perceive your actions as overstepping and unwanted. This is a risk that must be undertaken with great care, but to avoid long-term harm and unhealthy relationships, it is one that we must sometimes take.

I often think that "conflict avoidance" is one of the hardest life habits to break. This does not mean that people should engage in conflict for the sake of conflict. As a society, we have seemed to want everyone to "get along" so much that we have created behaviors that make that getting along superficial. I am a firm believer in the idea that it is through addressing tensions and conflicts and then handling them well that we discover new things about each other and grow as individuals and communities. When we fail to address these tensions and conflicts, they build up and become places of resentment that eventually explode in unhealthy and harmful ways.

Avoiding conflict is seductive. It lets you continue as before because you do not have to deal with conflict—for now. But not talking about something rarely makes the conflict go away.

An example of this that comes readily to mind in our country is race.

We have done a poor job as a culture and country talking about and addressing race and racism and its ramifications. No wonder that those who have felt left out or unheard have built up resentment that then manifests itself in institutional racism, poverty, and sometimes violence. Sure, we had a Black president, and the nature of our systems may on the surface look different than they did during the early parts of our country's life. But race still plays a major role in our people's conflicts, and we have not found a way to address it substantially. Unless and until we value the dignity of the other person, race will continue to divide us. Until we exchange our defensiveness and blaming for listening, empathy, and action, nothing will change, and we will all continue to suffer the consequences.

It is not kindness to avoid conflicts and difficult conversations with those close to you at work, family, school, and community. This culture of merely "getting along" and "not making waves" preserves the status quo. It allows resentments to fester, bad behavior to be rewarded, and pain to go unhealed. If you are like me, when something happens between me and someone else that must be addressed, this is my typical train of thought. (Not like I ever avoid conflict in my marriage to Robin…)

Well, that was not good, Robin is clearly upset with me.

I should see if she wants to talk.

After I check Twitter.

An hour later...

Hmm, seems like she is still upset. I'm definitely going to talk.

Whew, kids came home. Definitely after we eat dinner, then we'll talk.

The next morning...

Okay, after we all get home this evening...

I can keep this train going for a long time, until she or I simply can't take the tension any longer and we ask, "What's wrong?" or "Can we talk about...?" When the release valve is opened, almost all the tension and worry about what may happen is released. While most of our disagreements are exacerbated by hunger or project deadlines and can be healed with a few words of understanding or apology, there have been times when we had to have hard conversations about our relationship and life decisions. You and I both know that the sooner we tackle the conflict, the better—and the kinder.

So the next time there is a conflict, large or small, take a risk and address it. Risk stepping into the mess because, more times than not, on the other side of the tension there are new beginnings, strengthened relationships, and the knowledge that conflict is not something to avoid, but a means to a deeper, stronger, and kinder world.

For Reflection:
What current conflict are you avoiding addressing? Why?
When have you addressed conflict well? What was the result?

Try This:
Name a current conflicted situation that you are having with
a person, and commit to talking with them about it.

Kindness and
Those Closest to Us

SOMETIMES IT'S MOST difficult to be kind to the people who are closest to us.

I talk about Grandma Reyes quite a bit because she was such a complicated person. She lived on her terms, which I greatly admire. She was also stubborn, even to her death, which created hurts that will never be able to heal.

My grandmother was a deacon in our family's local church, Trinity Presbyterian Church in Stockton, California. Traditionally, deacons are the ones who take care of the people. They are often assigned duties like providing coffee and refreshments after church, praying for the community, and visiting people when they are sick or in the hospital. Grandma was a great deacon, except for the hospital part. She hated hospitals, though not for the reasons one might think. Some people don't like hospitals because the sickness and death are too much for them, others may be triggered by some event in their life where hospitals have been part of the experience, and still others avoid them because doctors are scary—yes, even with lollipops and stickers. Doctors. Scary.

None of these was the reason that Grandma Reyes avoided this particular deacon duty. She believed that whenever someone went to the hospital, they were waiting for a specific person to visit before they could allow themselves to die. Yep, my grandmother didn't want to be that person and be the reason that good ol' Uncle Connie decided to give up the ghost and go ahead and die. Did I mention that my grandmother had a very high sense of herself? It is hysterical and right in line with her personality. She was not taking any chances, so nope. No hospital visits for Deacon Marie.

This backstory is important because of the way my grandmother eventually died. My grandmother lived to be eighty-four, fueled the whole way by pork adobo and cigarettes. When we tried to get her to stop smoking in her seventies, she said to us, "Why? All I am saving are the last few years, and those years are the worst." Fair enough, Grandma.

Damn, I miss that lady.

As her life was ending, she was put on life support at a hospital in Stockton. When it became clear that she would not recover from her stroke, our family decided that it was time to remove her from life support—or rather, my mother and I decided, because the rest of the family was too scared of her ghost to make the decision. Ah, the life of eldest children. But I digress. We gathered everyone in the room. We circled around her. We had all said our goodbyes beforehand, so there we stood in silence as the nurse began to turn off the machines. Our dear stubborn and funny and now bloated and dying grandma was finally going to be able to rest.

Ha!

As a pastor, I have had the privilege of being with families during this challenging but liberating moment, and it never happens like in the movies. Once the machines are turned off, there is rarely a final, sweet breath and then death. There can be some struggle breathing, and the body may react in startling ways, but death does come.

Not for Grandma. At least not then.

Once the breathing machine was turned off and the tube removed from her throat, she kept on breathing.

And breathing.

And breathing.

All we could do was burst out laughing. It was the kind of laughter that happens during these times of deep communal grief. This was laughter born of weariness, given depth by sadness, and fueled by vending machine candy bars.

We laughed.

And we laughed some more.

Even now as I write this, I am still chuckling.

Once we knew that death would not be coming soon, we decided that my mother would stay with her that night, and the rest of the family could go home and rest if they wanted to. A handful of us stayed in the waiting room while my grandmother and her eldest child sat in the room together. Mom held her mother's hand, talked about her life, and told her stories of her grandchildren.

And then my mother remembered: someone who is dying is always waiting for a particular person to come before they can die.

With that, Mom leaned over her mother and whispered in her ear, "Mom, Dad's not coming."

And twenty minutes later, Grandma died.

I still get teary every time I recount this story, not only because it brings to life again the colorful personality of my grandmother, but because it reminds me of the dangers of not being kind to those who are closest to us.

For as amazing as my grandmother was, she was not kind to my grandfather, and eventually her actions created a rift that could not be repaired. My grandfather was a man who made amazingly kind and generous gestures toward my grandmother, but she was never able to own her part in much of the ugliness between them, nor seek reconciliation of any kind with my grandfather. I am not sure that my grandfather even knew that my grandmother was dying, as that was when he was with his third wife. If he had known and was able to come to her, my guess is that he would have, but he didn't. Still, in the depths of my grandmother's body, she apparently thought he might.

Often we are the least kind to those who are closest to us. Whether it is the proximity that does away with all kindness filters, an intimacy that makes us comfortable saying anything we want, or a lack of accountability to anyone, I know that I am often less kind to those around me than those far away.

Apologies to all close to me.

Vague blanket apologies published in a book they're unlikely to read is good, right?

Don't answer that.

So it's as well not to take for granted those closest to us. Sure, friends and family may be more apt to forgive when we are unkind, but drawing from that well too many times will easily create resentment and hard feelings. When it does happen, have the courage to apologize and find ways to repair the relationship. A genuine apology can go a long way.

Kindness, when it comes to those closest to us, is not simply about not being an idiot, but about consistently expressing kindness. Taking for granted those who are closest to us not only manifests itself in being unkind but also in forgetting to be kind. While there is undoubtedly an unspoken bond between close family members and dearest friends, kindness by osmosis is not an actual gesture of kindness. Actually making kind gestures is.

I know that I have to work on being kinder to my loved ones. I am horrible at remembering family birthdays, I do not check in with my mother as often as I should, and I know that I fall short time and time again with my wife.

Man, I am not a good person.

Never mind, scrap it all, you can be mean to those closest to you. Much easier.

Jokes, people!

We can certainly all try to be kinder to those closest to us to remind them that we genuinely value and appreciate them. Yes, that we value and appreciate them is what we are telling anyone when we are kind. The extra effort of stepping out of our daily routine of work, family, school, and connecting with a person through a kind act can be a powerful and tangible symbol of the bond that is assumed and cherished. Kindness extended and received will only deepen those bonds.

For Reflection:
When was the last time you were less than kind to
a person close to you?
What are ways that your friend group or family exhibits
kindness to one another?

Try This:
Think of one friend or family member whom you
have been meaning to call. Call them.

Kindness and the Public Square

I WILL NEVER forget where I was on election night 2016. This was one of the first elections processes in which my three children were truly engaged, and they were excited about the possibility of the United States having its first female president. We were all sitting on the couch as the results started rolling in, and as it became clear that Donald Trump was going to be elected president, I looked over and saw my youngest daughter weeping uncontrollably in her mother's arms.

My parental heart was torn, and the last thing I was feeling was kindness.

At that point, this would have been one of the most challenging chapters on kindness to write. My notes for the chapter looked like this:

- List names Trump has called his enemies.
- List instances of aggression and bullying.
- List instances of violent and dehumanizing rhetoric.
- List the lists of things at which he has been the best president ever.

But I did not give him either the time or the space. I leave that to Wikipedia.

Breathe, Bruce. Just breathe.

I am still not a Trump supporter. Contrary to what he shouted from the rooftops, his leadership style, his policies, and his behavior have not been some positive shakeup of a political system, but an attempt to destroy whatever fragile agreements society had about what was acceptable behavior within mainstream US culture and the global community. His term in office has redefined norms in ways that are not liberating. They have brought death and anguish to communities of color; have emboldened racist, misogynist, xenophobic, Islamophobic, and transphobic behavior; and have extolled dehumanizing, lying, and mockery as legitimate, valid, and even acceptable modes of human interaction.

He is not just a schoolyard bully; he is a bully with actual power.

What I do believe he has done is changed the unspoken rules and societal norms about how we engage with one another when it comes to disagreeing about just about everything under the sun: preferences, lifestyles, and politics.

"Hey, Feelings Fred, that avocado toast you are dripping on your hipster neckbeard is a gateway food to socialism, ten-dollar hemp vegan tacos, and wearing socks with Birks! Why do you hate America—and straws? You coddled, liberal-tears-crying, treasonous traitor!"

Or...

"Nice one, Ammunition Amy. That purity cross you are wearing clashes with your MAGA hat, and the only thing it is saving you from is acknowledging that your son and his Brown 'roommate' have sex, and they are not even married. Why do you hate love—and *Hamilton*? You faux-persecuted, white evangelical, right-wing nutjob!"

And while I am just kidding—or am I?—this is tame considering what most of us have seen and heard over these past years. The name-calling, the violence, the dismissiveness, the dehumanization; the pandemic press conference temper tantrums; the inability to admit that he was wrong; his fascination with TV ratings and his abuse of the media; his subtle and not-so-subtle misogyny, racism, and xenophobia—the list goes on and on and on.

Damn you, Donald Trump!

I mean, "I am very disappointed in you, Mr. Created and Complex Human Being, President Donald Trump."

Nope, not the same.

As part of a family that has always rigorously and publicly engaged in the political process, what we have become in the public square both makes my head want to explode with rage toward the cavalier ways we treat one another and makes my heart heavy with sadness and grief for what we have lost.

Yes, President Trump is an easy target, but there is collateral damage and other ways that this devolved and destructive rhetoric has become the norm. Dehumanizing is sinister and insidious because it provides short-term if not bankrupt feelings of power. It begins to shape the ways that we perceive ourselves and those around us. We begin to think that all that matters is what we have felt or experienced, and damn however this might impact anyone else. It gives authority and influence to the most outrageous, and worse yet it feeds the idea that the endgame is always victory over others or, at the very least, crushing our opponent's spirit into submission. To combat this new public square reality, we not only have to hold accountable the main perpetrator but also—and in many ways, more importantly—have to understand that this has now become a disease in our world.

Here are just a few examples.

Women and gender nonconforming people get the worst of this. When people come after me in a direct message, email, or comment, rarely is it about my looks or my love life. And never are sexually violent comments subtly or aggressively directed toward me. No, this misogyny is not new, but from the microaggressions that focus on women's bodies to outright threats of sexual assault, women have had to bear a great deal of the weight of this now acceptable way to engage in the public square.

This treatment also has a not-so-subtle homophobic tone as well, for any behaviors, relationships, or perspectives that do not ascribe to rigid understandings of maleness are somehow less than. This is one way in which men are often attacked using sexual violence, but again, it is built on the idea that the worst thing one can be is female.

So men, if your female colleagues don't take your "jokes" well, or you are challenged on your own language or lack of commitment to holding your male colleagues accountable, do you blame those women? While you may see and perceive actions as "not that big of a deal," many (most) know firsthand what comes next.

People of color, especially Brown and Black communities, seem to have borne the rest of the weight of this new rhetorical norm that has overtaken the public square. These communities have to deal with the public fetishism that makes theater of the actual violence perpetrated upon their bodies, the double standards of treatment by law enforcement and a disproportionate number of Black and Brown people incarcerated in the US prison system, and xenophobia that leads to scapegoating and the use of immigrants as political pawns. On top of all that, these communities also have to deal with white folks and self-proclaimed allies who want to make issues of race about themselves. As well intentioned as some white folks and other allies may be, they decenter the conversation off Black and Brown bodies and make it about them. This is often played out when "woke" white folks respond to a situation of racism by beginning with some version of, "I know what you mean. One time I was the only white person in the room, and…" This new rhetoric has so calcified sides that to call someone out on this behavior generates feelings of ingratitude at best and abdication at worst. If you are a white person who does this and are not sure why your Black friends react the way they do, maybe you should ask them. Wait, wait: again, if white people were truly in relationship with Black folks, you would not have to.

Okay, so how do we actually change the culture that has become so quickly and deeply rooted in our public and political discourse? Full confession: my wife and I did write a book titled *Rule #2: Don't Be an Asshat: An Official Handbook for Raising Parents and Children*, so I realize that I am standing on shaky ground here when it comes to falling into worn-out tropes about right-wing, gun-toting conspiracy theorists—darn, I did it again—thus contributing to the name-calling, demonizing, and bullying tactics that I am trying to fight. While I do blame President Trump for flinging wide the door to the worst of schoolyard bullying and assault, many on both the "left" or "right" have dipped their toes into that pool. After all, it does feel good to fire off that "You're an idiot" reply, to retweet that zinger meme, or to not even address the original statement and comment about something else altogether.

At the end of the day, I think most people during this time have become lazy in their critiques and engagement in public discourse and have, by osmosis or intention, taken on some of the very behaviors that this president is accused of exhibiting himself. We may blame it on character counts in a tweet or attention spans, but in any case, this way of interacting feeds ideological bloodlust and our need to vanquish our enemies. It's as if we're always bracing for some modern-day medieval-style siege that happens not at the gates of our castles, but on our screens.

Break out the metaphorical goblets of ale and turkey legs!

To be super clear: I am not drawing false equivalencies between the negative actions of the Democrats and Republicans, or the left and right, and so on. I do believe that if we were keeping score, the right is muuuuuuuuch more violent, abusive, and inciting than the left. Yes, we can all point to anecdotal evidence of the entire ideological spectrum behaving badly, so to play the "Who is worse?" game would be an exercise in futility. That said, I am fairly confident that *everyone*, at some point, has fallen victim to the seduction that is the sharing of that cutting tweet, funny meme, or snarky GIF, and has thus reinforced a political space that most values disrespect and dehumanization.

If you are with me that how we engage in the public square, both in person and online, has changed radically since that election day in 2016, the most important question becomes, *How can we be kinder?* For if kindness and the acknowledgment of the other's createdness extends to all people, then we must practice it in places where it is least evident. Otherwise, we join the unwinnable game of determining who is not worthy of human dignity.

The underlying questions, for me, are, *How can we be kind to those with whom we don't agree and still stand up for what we believe? How exactly do I do this?*

Whenever I am tempted to lash out, I now practice using a few kindness filters. I ask myself, *Would I be willing to say or share this in person?*

When it's not a face-to-face encounter but instead online, we tend not to reflect so much on making a scathing, mean-spirited comment. If someone calls us on it, we either abruptly fall silent or try to backpedal like a retired circus clown on a unicycle. Yes, I realize that some folks are using shock tactics in order to gain followers or to maintain a brand, or because they feel called to provoke, prod, and poke. Nonetheless, there's a wisdom in not giving in to the ease that is the protection of the screen.

I do not always succeed in this, but I am confident that if you scrolled through my Twitter feed, 98.45 percent of my tweets are things I'd also be willing to say to the person face-to-face. While rage and emotional release are essential for many of us, let's not get to the point that we no longer recognize that there is another human being on the receiving end of our comments.

Of course not everyone who is online engages with others. They lurk. This used to have connotations of Creeper McCreeperston, but now reading without reacting maintains some boundaries. With this in mind, whenever I post a tweet or update, I am actively thinking about the breadth of people who may read them. Some are looking for affirmation and encouragement about life, some are looking for information and new perspectives about politics, some are looking for community and interaction built on my brand of kindness, and a few are probably waiting for me to mess up so they can call me on my psychobabble.

I focus on the first three. These are the folks for whom I still share my thoughts on essential issues of the day in a way that I believe is worth my time and energy.

Am I reinforcing any culturally oppressive and excluding ideas?

Again, I am no fan of the forty-fifth president of the United States, nor do I believe that any first ladies have an obligation to be an extension of the presidency. That said, the body-shaming and misogyny that I have seen coming from otherwise kind people toward Donald and Melania Trump does nothing to build a case against the constant barrage of racism and misogyny that Barack and Michelle Obama had to endure. Left, right, progressive, conservative, RINO, Tea Party, Justice Democrats, Social Democrats, Socialist Democrats, Log Cabin Republican, or Blue Dog Democrats—I don't care that you hold passionate political views that others will stand in opposition to, but responses that are built upon the particulars of the person's appearance rather than assessments of positions do nothing to honor the human dignity of your enemy.

At the end of the day, dipping into the attack well of body-shaming, racism, misogyny, and ableism is just lazy. When people resort to these kinds of tactics, I simply think that they have lost the ability to debate the merits and content of a position. Instead, they want to play to the bot-fueled, troll-fed, worst of who humans can be. Seriously, if you cannot find anything else about President Trump to critique other than his hairstyle, skin tone, or weight, you are not trying that hard. Lastly and most importantly, for those who claim to be against these kinds of isms in society—I'm looking at all you recipients of the "liberal agenda"—we have to resist the temptation to fight evil with evil and honor the humanity of each person, enemy, ally, or friend.

Am I trying to engage or win?

Trying to hold in harmony all that life has to offer—work, family, health, school, friends, politics, society, love, coffee, chicken tikka masala, English bull terriers, baseball, having no mercy for my children at Settlers of Catan, watching the *Fast & Furious* franchise on repeat, and dreaming of Maui in retirement time (sorry, were those last few out loud?)—compels us to honor our time and energy. As I manage my public online time, I am acutely aware of this challenge and rarely give that time to trying to claim victory over another person.

Yes, I believe that all that I do is part of a movement toward an arc of justice, but on the one-to-one, I would much rather give energy and time to folks who are genuinely interested in engaging with one another. And I pay attention not only to those who agree with me but also to those who do not.

More times than I can remember, before I give my time to respond to some tweet reply, even if it's a passive-aggressive or caustic one, I will ask the tweeter, "Are you interested in engaging?" There have been a few times when I have had some fascinating interactions, but usually the other person goes radio silent. My guess is that they are like my pups when they have pooped in a shoe: "Oh darn. He noticed. Hide." Or they are just trolling the Twittersphere and couldn't care less.

At the end of the day, no one is entitled to your time, in person or online. You can choose to honor relationships, make sacrifices, and so on. But you are the one who must develop the discipline to regulate your time and energy spent in the public square—or might I suggest watching the *Fast & Furious* franchise on repeat.

For Reflection:
Share the last time you shamed a public figure. What was the context, was it helpful, and would you do it again? Where do you see the most shaming going on in your context?

Try This:
The next time you see a friend shame someone's body, intellect, or politics, call them out.

Kindness and the Everyday

I HAVE BEEN driving my kids to school every day for ninety-five years.

Okay, it's been more like seventy-four years.

Okay, sixteen years and counting.

One thing that I have noticed about drop-off culture is that we can be jerks at drop-off. I was tempted to title this chapter "We're all in a rush. You're not special. We're all going to the same place. You are an idiot." But that would not be kind, would it? Funny and true, but not kind.

My school drop-off battleground is one particular intersection in San Francisco. It is one of those streets where it starts as two lanes, and then it changes to where one lane is a forced right-turn lane and the other is a through lane. The battle begins if a car does not get into the through lane soon enough and finds itself trapped in a turn lane that has a solid line forbidding them to change lanes. Did you hear me, people? *Forbidding!*

I am seriously a work in progress.

As the years passed and my children found my ranting tiresome, I slowly began to change my mindset. Now as I approach that intersection, I find my inside voice calmly and soothingly reminding me, *Bruce, be kind and let them merge across the forbidden solid white line. You do not need to teach them a lesson. You do not own the land upon which your vehicle is traveling. Most importantly, you do not know what kind of a morning they are having. They might be in great need of a kind act. You are in a position to offer one.*

You think I'm joking, but I'm not. To this day, that conversation happens in my head when I am in any type of merging situation.

Yes, I'm exhausting.

The thing is, kindness is exhausting because most of us are not practiced or disciplined at living it, so we must choose to live kindness every single darn day. Kindness in our everyday lives does not just happen. It requires a deep commitment and practiced discipline of acting against so many of our natural reactions.

Every moment of every day, we have to choose if we will see the dignity of all people as we encounter them. This is especially true when it comes to the routine, everyday, monotonous acts of our lives. While grand gestures are great, especially one in re-action to events of urgency and tragedy, I fear that we use grand public gestures in order to shirk our responsibilities to the subtle and unknown things of life. You know, like school drop-off.

Here are my suggestions for five ways to be kind during school drop-off.

Let people merge. You do not actually own the land under your car, so their action is not some kind of hostile takeover of your royal estate. Chill. Let them merge. It will be fine.

Make legal U-turns. Please only make U-turns where they are allowed. This is generally not whenever you want and without any notice to those behind you. Making a legal U-turn will allow your car enough room to make the U-turn so you can avoid doing that awkward back up, go forward, back up, go forward move in front of all us.

Park and walk. For those of us who have some flexibility, one of the kindest things we can do is park our car away from the congested area and in a legal space and then walk with our kid or let them walk the rest of the way on their own. Not only does this give our body a moment to rest and exhale, but there is now one less car in the line. When you find yourself back in your car after the offspring have launched, take this as a ten-minute gift. Work on your Spanish, listen to the news, headbang to your favorite metal band, or lean that seat back and take a ten-minute power nap. When you wake, drop-off traffic will have subsided, and you can go on your way unstressed.

Restrain your honker. My straightforward rule when dropping off kids at school is "When within two miles of the school, do not honk at anyone." When I do honk in frustration, 99 percent of the time I'll discover I've honked at the parent of some kid we know, or I will later be in some parent gathering, and yep, they will be there.

Wouldn't it be great if all car horns had designated beep levels?

> Beep Level 1: "Hey there, I know you! How's it going?"

Beep Level 2: "Excuse me, just wanted to let you know that the light turned green!"
Beep Level 3: "Your coffee cup is on your roof."
Beep Level 4: "Hey, hey, hey, you are about to hit me!"
Beep Level 5: "Arrrgggggggghhhhhhh!"

As for any of you who have some cool new app or a fancy-pants car that already has this feature, yay you. For the rest of us driving cars old enough to have their own driver's license, until I level up my car game, I'm just laying off the honker.

Wave. While I do not believe a cute smile and a fluttering wave of the hand excuses bad drop-off behavior, a thank-you wave to the person who has shown you some vehicular kindness is much appreciated.

Besides school drop-off, there are other routines that can benefit from such kind responses. Imagine a kindness list for taking public transportation, cheering on the sideline, going to a movie, standing in line at the coffee shop, traveling on an airplane—you get my drift. These are small moments in our days, but such gestures of kindness spill over to our whole lives.

For Reflection:
Where do you find yourself struggling to be
kind on a regular basis?
How might a group or community normalize
and communicate everyday kindness?

Try This:
Unless you're in a situation of physical danger,
don't honk today.

Kindness and Institutional Change

I LOVE MEETINGS.

Wait. Let me rephrase that. I love well-run, meaningful meetings.

While I have done stints in the service industry, at a law firm, and in not-for-profit work, a majority of my working life has been working in religious institutions. I have moderated or facilitated meetings of just a few persons to ones of over a thousand, and I can tell you this: a well-run meeting can dramatically change the ways we experience one another and thus how much we will be committed to the community's purpose and life together.

So how does kindness fit into running meetings, you ask?

Many moons ago, when I was the pastor of a church with a congregation that was mostly young adults under thirty, we had monthly meetings of what is called a "Session," basically the board of directors of the church. In many churches, being on Session or the church council isn't generally the most life-giving and fun experience.

Rather than meeting around a conference room table or treating it as a business meeting, our Session met in our church "living room," and we each brought the food and beverage of our choice. We understood the purpose of Session to be one of mutual support and connection, a sacred task of leading other people in their spiritual journeys. Sure, we had to make decisions about budgets, building maintenance, and other things. But our true task was to be an extension of an experience that we were creating as a church, an experience that was life-giving and meaningful.

At one of those meetings, one person came up the stairs, arriving right after getting off work, and plopped down on one of our bright orange couches in the living room with a burrito and beer in hand. She exhaled deeply, then said, "I'm so glad to be at Session."

That moment affirmed in my mind that the culture that I was helping to create was one of meaning. It affirmed that if we honor and value the complex ways in which people engage in organizational work, we are honoring the person and showing them kindness. At the end of the day, kindness in a meeting environment is about valuing the human before us: their time, their perspectives, and their personalities.

I figure a chapter on meetings screams for a kindness agenda, so here goes.

Respect time. Set expectations for the time and honor the time committed. If you say you are going to start at seven, then do your best to do so. The more often you fudge the start time, the more people will begin to drag in later and later. This also goes for the end time. So if you find yourself approaching the agreed-upon ending time, check in with folks to find out whether going over is okay. If people need to check with support people in their lives or if you have to reschedule the meeting, do so. Be flexible, but also honor the time that folks have committed to give to the tasks at hand.

Create space. Ask yourself, *What does the room layout communicate to those who will be part of the meeting?* Rows of chairs or conference room tables send a different message to participants than couches or chairs in a circle. Neither is intrinsically better than the other, but make sure that your space makes sense for the kind of meeting you are going to hold. Also, for the love of all that is holy, make sure the space feels tended to as a symbolic way of letting people know that you will just as carefully tend to the people who attend and the topics you will address. Make sure the meeting space is easy to find, neat and tidy, appropriately heated or cooled, has sufficient seats, and (unless this is a no-tech meeting) that it has power strips within reach for charging phones and computers.

Be prepared. There are few things more frustrating than a leader or facilitator showing up unprepared. Yes, things happen in our lives that will disrupt even the most well-laid plans, and there will be times when we must ask for a little grace and flexibility, but do not make it a habit to wing meeting leadership. If you consistently show up unprepared to lead a meeting, not only are you signaling to participants and other leaders that it is all right if they are unprepared, but you are also not valuing the energy, time, and preparation that each person has brought into the space.

Honor personalities. Be intentional about honoring how people receive information and share opinions. If you are an extrovert like I am, not only can we be horrible listeners, always thinking about our response before the other person is done talking, but we also have a tendency to see space and fill it as fast as we can. While we process out loud and with others, the introverts in the room probably are shaking their heads. *There go the extroverts again. No, it's cool, you all are the only ones with anything of value to say. Not.* As an extrovert, when I am facilitating a meeting, I am super-intentional about requiring people to pause before answering a question. While the extroverts are like chained dogs ready to be unleashed on a pile of steaks, the introverts are given permission to exhale and take time to organize their thoughts before answering. Asking people to pause before answering makes for greater buy-in regardless of who is in change. Fellow extroverts: I promise that if you do not get to talk first and the most today, you will be okay.

Focus on strengths. Meetings that focus on abundance and the gifts that people bring to the space are so much more motivating than meetings that are filled with a focus on scarcity and what cannot be done. Addressing obstacles and determining common directions will find more success if done with a lens of positivity and possibility rather than pessimism and resignation.

Maintain focus. In my twenty-plus years of running meetings, the gift that I have most honed is the ability to guide people gently and appropriately back to the topic at hand. Sometimes people will resent not being able to overrun the meeting completely, but everyone else will be appreciative. Maintaining focus is not about silencing voices, but about honoring the energy and focus people are directing toward a particular topic. When drawing people back to the topic at hand, always be sure to create space for the other topic to be taken up in the future. As this kind of focus becomes part of the culture of your organization, others will begin to trust not only that you will make decisions thoughtfully but also that all voices will be heard—just not all at the same time.

Avoid surprises. People don't like them. Even what may seem like no-brainer surprises (like the gift of a car, vacation, or puppy) have their attendant issues and complexities. When it comes to meetings, unexpected crises are one thing, but surprises that are the result of a lack of preparation or that are a deliberate tactic to rush to a decision without meaningful conversation are quite another. It is so tempting to believe that a new thing will not be that big of a deal, but even the most flexible of us can only take so much unexpected change. Postponing a decision until the next meeting to make sure everyone has a chance to give input can create frustration, but over the long haul, by honoring the multitude of voices, you are creating buy-in and honoring each individual involved.

Read the room. Being unable or unwilling to read the room is usually due to an overcommitment to the agenda and an unwillingness or inability to be flexible. This typically takes two forms: one is when the group is clearly ready to make a decision, yet the leader allows the discussion to go on and on; the other is when the group is clearly not prepared to make a decision, but the leader plows through anyway instead of taking the time to build consensus and allow for each person's buy-in. In both cases, the facilitator needs to be firm in moving things along or encouraging more conversation. Both responses allow for a more productive meeting and confidence in the person running the meeting.

Oh, wait: there is a third, necessary room-reading skill—bathroom breaks.

Invite feedback. While most of us do not really want feedback—unless we know it's going to along the lines of "Bruce is the most amazing person ever!"—asking for feedback is always helpful. I try to end meetings with a few versions of the following questions:

> "What went well during our meeting? What was helpful?"

> "What would have been more helpful?"

> "How could I have been more helpful in facilitating the meeting?"

Though it can hurt (briefly), knowing how others experience our leadership means that we can adjust or stop using practices that are not so helpful.

Have fun. Even the most difficult meeting, when done well, can be meaningful and life-giving. From the most severe issues to the seemingly innocuous ones, decisions are rarely neutral in impact. Whether you are dealing with something as important as a personnel decision or something as mind-numbing as who should have access to the photocopier codes (true story), how we handle these decisions can help build up or tear down the community. For instance, if I had called the conversation about the copier code "mind-numbing" at the time, that would not have been helpful. Clearly someone in the room felt it was an important conversation to have.

Just because meetings will always be a part of life, that does not mean that they have to be deadly. When run well, they can give us a positive, collective purpose; an energy about movements for change; and a sense of fulfillment that we are using our time, energy, and skills in meaningful ways.

All in favor, please say aye :-)

For Reflection:
Think of the last "good" meeting you attended.
What made it good?
What is the next meeting you will lead, and how might you adjust your meeting practices having read this chapter?

Try This:
To alleviate surprises and mitigate anxiety-producing urgency, encourage all decisions to be given a first read well ahead of decision time.

Kindness and Resistance

In 2018, along with about thirty other religious leaders, I was arrested at the US-Mexico border as part of an action to bring visibility to the militarization of the border and the cruelty of the US immigration system. Despite the militaristic intimidation, testosterone-fueled chest-beating, and physical nature of the actual arrest, what stuck with me is kindness. No, neither Border Patrol nor Homeland Security agents acknowledged that we were beautifully and divinely created humans. Rather, sitting in the back of the police van cuffed and crowded together with friends old and new, humanity reigned. Old and young; Muslim, Christian, and Buddhist; white, Brown, and Black; newbies to civil disobedience and veterans to troublemaking laughed and commiserated together. We genuinely got to know one another as people, individually created beautiful human beings.

I am one of those people who has pretty much never encountered a protest that I did not want to attend. My family and religious roots have taught me to show up, speak up, and shine light upon unjust systems. I have attended radical actions, I have organized public actions, and I have participated in mainstream marches. I have been struck by police batons and feared for my body, I have been arrested gently and wondered how this could be called protest, and I have been arrested forcefully and have wondered whether I would be hustled off to some secret Homeland Security facility.

I believe that active, persistent, and public resistance is crucial to the success of any and all movements for change.

Because I am committed to active resistance and because we often think of the fight for social justice causes as aggressive, even sometimes violent, I know that this may be one of the more difficult places to see the power of kindness. Protests, marches, sit-ins, civil disobedience, even riots—all play a part in achieving justice and equality in the world. Without the voices from the edges publicly demanding, wailing, and protesting, institutions and systems that engage in exclusionary, oppressive, or marginalizing practices continue to operate with apathy or impunity. Destructive systems do not change themselves, and those working for change within these systems can't do it alone.

It is not surprising that, when faced with oppressive and violent situations, people have a hard time seeing kindness as a valuable and practical response. Certainly anger and rage are justified reactions in response to acts of injustice and oppressive systems. Yet anger and rage are not sustainable or life-giving over the long haul. Not only do we run the risk of escalating a culture of violence and retribution, but time and time again I have seen how anger can change the way people interact with those closest to them. Such anger typically comes not from righteous indignation but from unexpected burnout, a lack of self-awareness, and the burden of constant oppression and frustration. Anger and rage have their place. But at some point, we have to find ways to channel that rage and anger into actions that advance movements for equality and justice.

In the journey toward justice, no matter what issue is being confronted—ableism, xenophobia, misogyny, homophobia, racism, militarism, et cetera—it takes multiple tactics and perspectives to achieve just results. When the time is right for each of us, we must embrace actions and responses that recognize the humanity and dignity of the other, no matter how heinous the act that we are addressing.

Public protest, political resistance, and the fight for social justice are not just about confrontation. Here are a few ways in which I view kindness as part of that work.

Violence and aggression: Self-defense is one thing, but at the end of the day, I am committed to nonviolence. I understand why some reach a different conclusion and, like Martin Luther King Jr., see riots and other outbreaks of violence as expressions of pent-up frustrations and being unheard. But violence as a primary tactic does not value the human dignity of the other that is required of a posture of kindness. If I believe that my liberation can only come from your death, then what does that say about my liberation? Yes, there are horrible players in the world, both individual and institutional, who deserve to be locked away, dismantled, or removed from a place of power, but doing so through violence is not something I can support. This is not Pollyannaish or naive. Quite the opposite: kindness is a more difficult path because it requires us, first, to believe that each and every person has value and deserves to be seen as a created being and, second, not to let anger, hatred, or violence win the day.

Communal experience: As in my experience of being arrested at the border, one of the powerful outcomes of protest is community. Most of us who have been involved in these kinds of actions in the past know that the community-building component is real. Even so, we sometimes lapse into behaviors that are anything but kind. Sometimes our passions morph into purity tests, our egos take precedence over the good of the community, and we begin to think that the entire endeavor is all about us. The embodiment of kindness as part of these kinds of actions requires us to see one another as complex and created human beings who also happen to hold common political, ideological, or religious views. When we are able and willing to do this, movements become bonded by relationships and a depth of common purpose, thus giving the movement power and focus that would otherwise elude us.

Acts of civil disobedience: Not everyone has the space or privilege to participate in acts of civil disobedience. Because of life situations, immigration status, or other factors, there are many people who would be more than willing to engage in civil disobedience but would pay a price greater than many others to do so. Civil disobedience is not the only way we can push for greater social justice.

That said, if you ever are able to participate in civil disobedience and risk arrest, you will find that the training is done with a lens of kindness and humanity: yours, that of law enforcement, and that of everyone else who is involved. Not only will you be trained not to provoke, but you will also be trained that the heart of the act is to highlight the plight of human beings. When it comes to responding to law enforcement personnel, we focus on not reacting with violence no matter how much the system encourages them to try and provoke an aggressive act toward them. In this act, we are saying to those before us that we are all more than what the system wants us to be seen as or how the system wants us to behave—and we will act accordingly. In holding firm to such nonviolence, we force those who are acting as agents for the system to see us as human beings and question what they are doing rather than see us as ideological opposition that can be treated with detachment and disregard.

Spark is important, but kindness will sustain. Every person has a role in movements for justice and change. Some are thinkers, others are agitators, others are relationship builders, and still others work from within the system. There is a time and place for all who are in these struggles, but for those who are at the forefront of the protests, I know that sparks such as protests are only as effective and powerful as the systemic societal changes that come out of them. In this regard, kindness toward one another and valuing the role that everyone has in the movement is crucial. Yes, those with common goals must hold one another accountable for our actions and impact on people, but we must also hold with care the bigger picture and process of change. As we engage in this work over a lifetime, we will at some point find ourselves on both sides of the "move faster" or "be patient" divide. Though it is frustrating while we are in the thick of things, the power lies in us all needing each other in order for real change to happen. So rather than seeing coconspirators as those who have oppositional tactics and are not worthy of our time, empathy, or support, we must take comfort in the knowledge that these diverse tactics are fueled by our common passion for justice, making our individual tactics that much more powerful in combination with theirs.

There will always be injustice in the world, because, you know, humans. The question is how we will choose to respond to the injustice around us. There will be days on which the onslaught of news that highlights political nonsense, moral depravity, and human tragedy is overwhelming and makes it seem as if our efforts are useless, like trying to empty a sinking boat with a thimble. During these times, the choice to give in and give up will be tempting, especially for those of us who sit in positions of social, cultural, or economic privilege. It's tempting to throw our hands up in resignation, to turn our backs on the suffering of others, and to adopt an "every man for himself" mentality.

Please do not choose this.

For those who see no use in doing anything different because the world always has and always will be filled with awfulness, I say, "But can you imagine how much worse it would be if some people had given up along the way?" Yes, the world does seem like a constant dumpster fire fueled by racism, xenophobia, misogyny, greed, and so on. But as we look back on the previous generation's struggles, we realize that in many ways we have moved forward. Some of the gains have been short-lived, and context matters greatly. Even so, things would be much worse if those called to the work of social justice had simply given up. There will be times when the steps of progress seem small. Please remain in the struggle, recommit to the struggle, or join the struggle for the first time. Kindness, and the commitment to see the other as deserving of human dignity, demands of us to protest, resist, and do all that we can to fight that which says otherwise. Not only do we have the power to make sure that things do not get worse, but over the long haul, we also have the power to make long-lasting change for good.

I need you.

We need one another.

We can only do this together.

For Reflection:
When have you seen individual kindness embodied
in the context of public protest?
How might organizers ensure that their actions do not
reinforce or encourage acts that dehumanize, demean, or
dismiss the humanity of those who are the target of the action?

Try This:
If you have never been to a protest, go.
At your next public action, take a moment to get to know
someone else's story.

Kindness and Walking Away

My mother has been married three times. To put it bluntly, her first two marriages were disasters, and I am grateful that she chose to leave her first two husbands when she did. Looking back, I am not surprised that she has the strength and courage to make her own choices. This is a woman who had an unplanned kid right after graduation (yes, I was nicknamed "Boo Boo" unironically; no, really, it's fine) and was basically kicked out of her parents' house at eighteen to fend for herself.

I have much to say about the ups and downs of my relationship with my birth father as well as the lifesaving impact that my stepfather and my mom's husband for the past thirty years has had on my life, but I'll save both of those for my tell-all memoir dropping in 2056. Until then, I'm just going to spill tea about my stepfather David. After divorcing my birth father soon after I was born, my mother married David. Their marriage lasted from 1971 to 1979, and there were, of course, some good things about him—though I cannot think of one at this moment. In the end, he was just a jerk with a whole lot of issues. And while he wasn't married for very long to my mother, David has had an enormous influence on my life because he provided the backdrop for pretty much everything in my life in the 1970s. From the way we lived, to the makeup of our family, to the ways I understood fatherhood, David's imprint, like it or not, is there. I don't find myself fighting my David shadow as much as I used to, but there are times when I'm worried that I might become like him.

Most of what I remember about David are mental photographs of what I think happened. I thank God for a brain that sometimes forgets traumatic events that simply shouldn't have happened. Somehow our minds can block out those things. There was the time when I was five years old, and he told me I could get out of the car if I didn't listen to him. It would have been one thing had we been in the driveway of our house, but nope. We were on the freeway when he pulled over, opened the door, and I, at five years old, had to get out. Walking down the freeway, my mother in hysterics, I was not going to let him get the best of me. Now, it is one thing to play discipline chicken with a stubborn five-year-old; it is quite another to put him out of the car on the freeway and tell him to walk.

Then there are the countless times when I got in trouble for who knows what, and I had to take my punishment. I cannot imagine saying to my child, "Pull down your pants," as I take off my belt, and then striking her, over and over and over again. To say that "it hurts me more than you" is nonsense. To strike your child so hard with a belt on bare skin that you leave welts and marks is child abuse. I have heard many people share stories of similar beatings in households that would surprise you. The instruments may be different—a switch, clothes hanger, or wooden spoon—and the reasons may differ—bad grades, dirty room, or lying—but the fact remains that beating your children is not acceptable. It does not build character. It does not instill respect. All it does is reinforce the idea that the parent will "guide" their child with pain and fear rather than by taking the time to earn respect and love. The worst part is that you, the victim, then "gift" your children with a lifetime of having to deal with such "parenting" lessons and trying not to repeat this warped sense of what it means to raise children.

But it was not just me that David treated this way. I once saw him beat up his own brother—yes, in front of me—and then try to run him over with his car. David's antenna was bent during the altercation, so my uncle was left with bruises on his body and a bill for the antenna repair.

Quite the winner.

I am not sure if he ever physically assaulted my mom. I know he was emotionally abusive, and I saw how his fury would boil over toward me, so I would not be at all surprised if he had struck my mother.

And yet my mother had the courage to walk away from him.

Because, as we have learned and she has probably learned about herself, "Lola" (the Filipino word for grandmother) is a badass. I say this not only because she's my mom and will probably read this book but also because she has the street cred to prove it. While I am sure that Lola was quite the rabble-rouser as a teenager, she honed quintessential badassery as an adult:

Lola worked for the California state legislature for 25 years; then
Lola earned her undergraduate degree at age 40; then
Lola ran a high school truancy and drug prevention program; then
Lola earned her *first* master's degree at age 44; then
Lola earned her *second* master's degree at age 50; then
Lola pastored a Presbyterian church for 19 years; then
Lola earned a doctoral degree at age 60; then

Lola retired, though as I write this book, she has not really stopped working.

Oh, and along the way, she remarried, had two more kids for a total of four, has helped raise nine grandchildren and counting, and has over time welcomed many more adults and kids to the family table.

Like many people who show this kind of grit, you had also better not cross her. She has an Olympic gold medal in holding grudges and can be cuttingly mean at times—both traits passed down to her children.

Thanks, Mom.

More times than I can count, I have seen her call out people for their behavior, name injustice, and overall make everyone uncomfortable by refusing to let lousy behavior pass without challenge. *Silent, submissive,* and *pushover* are not words that describe my mother, and the world and those she has loved are better for it.

But she also has a tender side. Her kids can make her cry by simply being in the same space and saying, "I bet Mom is going to cry now." And yes, we do that. Like any parent, her heart aches when her children suffer emotionally, spiritually, or physically. So while she presents as tough, I also know that there is a part of her that loves too much. Knowing this about her makes the fact that she was able to extricate herself from two marriages probably the most courageous thing she has ever done, for her own sake and the sake of her children.

Thank you, Mom.

What I have learned from her is that sometimes we are most kind to ourselves and others if we disengage from those things that cause our body, mind, and spirit pain—and walk away.

I am so grateful that my mother had the courage to leave David. This definitely showed kindness to herself, because she recognized her own humanity and was able to honor that. But she also showed kindness to me and my sister. I am so grateful and relieved that David is no longer in our lives.

Walking away sometimes makes you think that you are giving up or are not sufficiently committed. In abusive relationships like this, you can be guilted into staying in these situations or manipulated into believing that the entire situation was your fault in the first place. In such situations, it is easy to recognize why walking away is an act of self-kindness and self-preservation. But even in less intense relationships that are no longer healthy or meaningful, sometimes the kind thing to do for everyone is to walk away, at least for a time.

The need to walk away occurs also in the domain of politics, and more than ever in the era of Donald Trump. But not everyone would agree that it's best to hold your tongue and not rock the boat. Instead, some people have gone all in talking about politics or religion in company of all kinds. In all kinds of situations, letting things go for the sake of being polite or nice can be dangerous to one's own self and can reinforce harmful attitudes that lead to destructive behavior.

In my experience, such interactions also often take place on the sidelines of kids' soccer games. This is a place where you are guaranteed to have people gathered who have a variety of personalities and hold differing perspectives. I have seen parents from opposing teams almost come to blows, I have heard racist comments about players, and I have seen parents blatantly drinking booze and acting the fool. Sometimes I said something, and at other times I just walked away and tried not to get caught on the inevitable "parents brawl at twelve-year-olds' soccer game" YouTube video.

And then there was the time I did both: in the midst of a quickly deteriorating situation, I walked away and avoided internet fame.

I still remember it so vividly. It began with a casual discussion of students walking out of school in protest of President Trump, and one parent's response, "Protesting is the dumbest thing ever. It is a complete waste of time." I really should have known better, but I didn't. I kept engaging the parent by saying I was proud of our kids standing up for what they believed.

The other parent would not let it go, and eventually we got to the real reason he believed it was a bad idea to protest Trump. Paraphrased, but not exaggerated, he said of Trump's presidency, "If you are gay, an immigrant, or a woman, it's going to suck, but if you are in the financial world, he is going to be great!"

At that point I thought my head was going to explode. This "liberal" person had just admitted that oppression was okay since he was going to make money from it. This is also the point at which I said, "X————, I need to walk away. We are done." But he kept at it. He desperately wanted me not to label him a Trump-supporting idiot, so he kept saying things like, "I don't agree with him, but what are we going to do?" I wanted to say, "Hmm, maybe protest whatever you think is so horrible—like our kids have been doing?" But I did not. Instead, I walked away. I think this was the kind thing to do.

It's okay to walk away rather than battle it out. When you believe that you are harming your own humanity, please walk. Tend to your long-term health and power of your being, as my mother did. Your physical, emotional, and psychological well-being deserves the same kind of dignity, care, and compassion that you are trying to extend to others. When it is not offered to you, you must claim it for yourself.

For Reflection:
When have you walked away from a situation as a gesture of kindness to yourself?
How can we help one another recognize when it is time to walk away from situations that may be detrimental to our emotional or physical health?

Try This:
If there is a person who you think needs to walk away from a situation, find a caring way to accompany them as they decide whether it is time to walk away.

Kindness and Forgiveness

WHEN MY DAUGHTERS were playing a ton of soccer, we noticed something interesting: they and their teammates apologized a lot. They apologized to their own teammates after making an errant pass, they apologized to the opposing player after a physical play, and they apologized to their coaches even when they didn't need to. Now, of course not everyone had this perspective. There is lore that my youngest child told a teammate, "Don't apologize, just make a better pass next time." But it got so bad that during one game, all the way from the other side of the field we heard their coach yell at them, *"Stop apologizing!"*

I'm not sure if male players have the same attitude on the field, and I am in no way encouraging bad sportspersonship, but the coach's point was that the time you took to look back and say sorry gave the other team the advantage. As my girls grew older, the apologies stopped, but I will never forget that voice from afar telling them to stop apologizing. It went against all that they were being taught in the rest of their lives: "When you make a mistake, apologize."

Making a genuine apology is difficult. If you are genuinely sorry and express remorse, you are admitting to yourself and to the one you wronged that you are not perfect and that something you did hurt or offended them. No one wants to admit that they screwed up.

With this in mind, from Bruce's Greatest Hits of Miscues and Foibles, here are some examples of times that my actions required heartfelt apologies:

- After being reminded multiple times that someone's preferred pronouns were *they/them*, I misgendered them more than once during a meeting. Thankfully, when I apologized, they acknowledged that I had corrected myself at the time and that reaching out was meaningful to them.
- After listening to a particularly good sermon by a female colleague, when I bumped into her after the service, I stupidly commented on her shoes before complimenting her on her sermon. Yes, we were friends; yes, her shoes were super cool. But given how often women receive comments about their hair, their shoes, and the timbre of their voices rather than their intellectual contributions, what the hell, Bruce? What. The. Hell. I later apologized and learned that she hadn't even noticed. The whole incident was troubling on many levels. But still, what the hell, Bruce?
- The many times I have overreacted to something my kids said or did. I try to apologize for my snark, raised voice, or disproportionate emotional response.

What does kindness look like in the face of acts for which people must be held accountable? This is one of the most challenging questions. Our society tends to value transactional relationships above all and often defaults to an "eye for an eye" retributive way of responding to wrongdoing. What role does forgiveness have in being kind?

The person who is wronged does not have to extend forgiveness to the perpetrator. Yet if the wronged person is genuinely interested in creating a space where some healing can take place, *and* the one who seeks forgiveness is genuinely remorseful, kindness will help create and tend that space.

While the examples that I gave above were real and genuine opportunities to exercise my apology muscle, I also know that there are levels of "wrongs" inflicted upon people and that my examples were relatively trivial. Our mistakes and offenses run the gamut from the seemingly small to the shockingly tragic, and thus our apologies must encompass this range of wrongdoing. Our world is not short of victims and tragedies. From sexual and physical violence (#MeToo) to malfeasance on a massive scale (Enron) and institutionalized injustice inflicted upon groups of people (like internment of Japanese Americans, enslavement of Africans in America, and Native American genocide), apologies take very different forms and operate at different scales.

I want to be very careful not to equate my commenting on a colleague's shoes before commenting on her sermon to the mass incarceration of Japanese Americans during World War II. They are not equivalent, not at all, and the apologies due each person or group harmed should take very different forms. At the same time, I do not want to make light of the small things that we do that often mark the beginnings of relationship resentment and give permission for offenders to trivialize any injuries inflicted upon another as insignificant or inoffensive.

Good or appropriate apologies for any scale of offense have some common attributes: they take genuine ownership of the wrongdoing, are offered without expectation of a response, and are focused on the victim and not the perpetrator.

Bad or insufficient apologies usually begin with some form of "I'm sorry that you were offended," or "I'm sorry that my actions made you feel this way." Neither takes responsibility for the action. In fact, it lays the onus for the offense on the victim. Known as gaslighting, or making the victim believe that it was their fault to begin with, this is one of the most common ways people apologize. If you do this, your apologies are meaningless, and you are only revictimizing the other.

Do not do this.

An apology that is truly meaningful makes no assumption and has no expectation of reconciliation. It is not transactional. It is simply one's admission of having committed a wrong. Forgiveness is not a "get out of relationship jail" card. Apologies are often part of the healing of any relationship, but depending on the offense, to apologize while assuming one will be forgiven and accepted makes the apology hollow. It puts the focus on the perpetrator and not the victim. When we do this, we retraumatize someone and make reconcilation that much more of a distant possibility.

Genuine apologies that are fueled by kindness are ones that honor the dignity of each person: yourself and the other. Excuses built on kindness say to the one offering the apology that, in order to grow, we must acknowledge that none of us is perfect; that sometimes—well, often—we mess up; and that we can change our ways. For the other, it is a gesture that affirms what they have experienced—namely an acknowledgment of damage done to them and an offer of future change.

Truly examining how and when we should apologize is complex. The opening vignette of my daughters on the soccer field reminds us that girls and women have been socialized to apologize. Not so for boys and men, for whom apologizing is often perceived as weakness. And while I do believe that this has shifted for many, one need look no further than popular culture and most political battles to see that toxic masculinity is alive and well in American culture. That said, for some cultures, shame and saving face are essential elements of relationships, and apologizing or calling someone out publicly creates other issues and problems. I raise all of these illustrations of the practice and perceptions of apologizing not as a prompt for us to apologize less or more, but to point out that, like most of life, apologies are filled with complexities, obstacles, and realities that must be navigated.

Genuine apologies are never easy to offer. Nor should they be, because apologies give voice to part of our personhood that needs to change and grow. We are admitting that we are not perfect, not a finished project. So whether you're nine or ninety, change of behavior, growth of self, and potential forgiveness, while difficult, make the endeavor and struggle worth it.

For Reflection:
How would you describe and assess the last time
you apologized to someone?
Name apologies that you have witnessed that were
(a) hollow or (b) meaningful.

Try This:
Reflect on a wrong that you have done to someone,
no matter how small, and offer that person an apology.

Kindness and Saviorism

Iɴ 2009, ᴀs part of a relief work delegation, I visited Haiti after a major earthquake. As we traveled through Port-au-Prince and the surrounding areas, we were confronted with dissonant visions: complete devastation of buildings and structures side by side with people engaged in recovery, life, and community.

When you see such traumatic situations firsthand, it is difficult not to shift into rescuer and savior mode. Those of us who grew up in countries that have a history of colonizing others are afflicted with a kind of colonizer hangover that often reveals itself during times of disaster and tragedy. With good intentions, we jump right in and attempt to rescue, fix, and save those who are in pain. The impulse to offer healing to those who are in pain is of course praiseworthy. But we should beware of "good intentions" clouded by the assumption that we know best how to respond to the situation: what people need, what people are capable of doing, and what we don't even know that we don't know. The ironic thing is that it is often when we are trying the hardest to see the other as a created being that we most deny the intricate creations that humans are. We one-dimensionalize, assume a lack of agency, and generally treat those in tragedy as eager recipients of any help that we can offer, whether or not our help is actually wanted or indeed helpful.

At no other point during my trip was this as obvious as when we stopped at a hospital that had been damaged and was being rebuilt. During the tour of the hospital, we were brought to a nondescript door at the end of the hallway. The director of this hospital swung the door open and, with the enthusiasm of guests being announced at an old-timey English ball, said, "I give you the room we call 'Junk for Jesus.'"

What greeted us was a huge room packed ceiling to floor with boxes—stuff that well-meaning but misguided and ill-informed churches had been sending this hospital in Haiti.

There were boxes of winter clothes, broken toys, and other things that were clearly more about cleaning out someone's basement than genuinely finding ways to help support, uplift, and rebuild this hospital. It was an example of guilt giving and lazy philanthropy, and while laughable in so many ways, it was also tremendously sad. This room represented an ongoing colonial mindset that most Christians from the United States still carried concerning Haiti and its people: not only can we decide what they need, but what we send them will be our leftovers. And even for such leftovers they should be grateful to us. Look, we did something! Our obligation has been fulfilled.

So frustrating.

Most of the fifty or so large boxes contained extra-large paper hospital gowns. This was the last thing that this hospital needed. First, extra-large gowns are huge, and second, paper hospital gowns in such a sweat-inducing climate are not durable. But to our chagrin and joy, they were being used—to produce charcoal! The hospital was giving them out to provide people with a heating source for cooking, water purification, and bathing.

I am trying to imagine the thank-you letter:

Dear First Church of Church City,

Thank you for the donation of the supplies.

We burned them.

In Christ, The Hospital.

Kindness that is fueled by guilt, pity, or colonialism is not kindness at all. Kindness is not currency or a commodity to be used to barter and bargain away the sins of our past or to alleviate our responsibility to be part of global recovery efforts in times of tragedy. Instead, when attempting to help others, kindness compels us to see the other as a complex human with agency and perspective. Kindness allows us to ask what is needed, provide support that is healthy, and enter into a relationship that is not patronizingly transactional in nature but relationally reciprocal in actuality. When we do this, we learn from one another, and we build up the wholeness of each human being as we journey our way into the future together.

For Reflection:

Name and talk about a time that you offered service to others.
When groups engage in service, how can you avoid being
patronizing?

Try This:

The next time there is some kind of support drive, think about
what you are offering and consider whether you are giving
your leftovers or responding to the recipients' stated needs.

Kindness and
the Internet

ROSEANNE ONCE TROLLED me.
    Okay. A little background.

In 2008, I was elected to the office of moderator of the Presbyterian Church (USA), at that point a denomination of just over one million members. The role required me to moderate our annual meeting of about one thousand people and then travel the country and the world on behalf of the denomination. For our church, this was a big deal. The pride of my family, home church, and mentors was overflowing. At that time, there was a resurgence of interest in our denomination by folks under forty. One of their own had been elected to this office, and—gasp!—he knew how to use the internet.

I had an opportunity to model a different way of being.

This also happened just prior to the 2008 presidential election, and the Presbyterians had just elected this young, tech-savvy leader who would usher in a new generation of ideas. So Barack, Michelle, Malia, Sasha, and America: You're welcome. Anytime you need me to pave the way for you again, just text me.

I make light of the relative notoriety of the office of moderator, but actually I'm not meaning to downplay those who had helped pave the way for me to be elected. Yet no one outside of the true church-nerd Presbyterian types really cared about my election. The title "moderator" alone triggers nap time, Presbyterian or not. I am sure if the title had been something like "His Royal Highness of St. Badassery" or, for you *Friends* fans out there, some form of "Princess Consuela Banana Hammock," my renown would have been global. Instead, my children once described to their friends why I traveled so much: "My dad is very important to a very small group of people."

Never was a more true statement offered to the universe.

And then there was the day I got this tweet directed at me; it has since been deleted.

 Roseanne Barr @therealroseanne   14m
@RabbiKenCohen Inspired by this hilarious play on words, I'll say: @breyeschow Chow looks like he loves 2 chow 2 much. #GA222 #Gluttony=Sin.

This was tweeted out during a meeting of the General Assembly of the Presbyterian Church (USA) being held in Portland, Oregon, in the summer of 2016. This tweet was one of a long thread of hate-filled rants regarding a debate we were having about divesting from companies who were profiting from nonpeaceful pursuits in the Middle East. Often framed as an Israel/Jewish-versus-Palestine/Muslim battle, this was not the first time someone had come at me about this particular issue.

But Roseanne? Yep.

Soon the shock of being trolled wore off. Folks soon realized that she did not deserve special treatment, and people began taking her to task for the ways that she interacted with me and others. In the end, while I was put on blast, there was no Roseanne army on my doorstep, and the buzz slowly faded away.

I have lots of stories about being attacked via the interweb. I've received threats of violence, shaming of all kinds, racist remarks, and the like. Yet, beyond the bots and other technological disruptors, and beyond the many people out there who find joy in tearing down other people, the vast majority of my online life has been positive and healthy.

I know that this is not everyone's experience, and those who occupy more marginalized lands have it much worse than I do. Everyone has the opportunity and obligation to try and create the kind of space that is supportive and generative and builds community. To help create this space for myself, here are a few filter questions I ask as I think about my online life.

Is this worth it? Here, I am not asking about respectability politics of tone-policing but merely about whether this is the right thing to post at this moment or on this topic. I am all about freedom of speech, but freedom of speech does not come with freedom from consequences. So I am always asking myself this question because, seriously, the blowback is just not worth the time and energy. This also is a good filter question when someone posts an opinion about something with which I simply disagree. I might question your getting all worked up about the return of pumpkin-spiced anything, or I may judge your utter lack of appreciation for a certain musical about a certain Founding Father played by a certain performer whose name might rhyme with "Din Danuel," but I do not have to post about it.

No matter how misguided some opinions maybe, I do not have to be the purveyor and filterer of all truth in the world, and sometimes my inside voice needs to stay right where it is: inside.

Whose voice is being amplified? One of the best parts about social media is the ability to amplify one another's views and voices, especially the voices of those on the margins of the political, cultural, or social landscape. Social media is inherently about the self; I ask the questions to make sure that my social media life is not entirely about me. I use my platform to bring some of the brilliance and beauty out there into the worldview of others, not as a "discovery" (that would make it about me again), but only as a nod to the fact that I do not need to be, nor am I good at, all things.

Am I 'splaining? Once a white person tried to correct my understanding of what it meant to be Asian American. Um, okay. Do you know to whom you are talking? Commonly known as "'splaining," this is when one person attempts to correct or inform another person about something, assuming that the other knows absolutely nothing about the subject already. I try not to answer questions that, first, no one asked and, second, I was never asked to answer, for by answering I assume that I actually know about everything and that I know more than anyone else.

Am I one-dimensionalizing? Oh, it is so easy for me to just jump on the "That person is a caricature" train and strip away any sense of complexity or human dignity that they may have. Yes, people must be held accountable, but in our critique of someone, we must always remember that each and every person is a complex and created human being. Yes, we must hold people accountable for their actions and words, but to be kind, our accountability must focus on actions and words and not question the very nature of who they are as a human being.

Am I letting myself be reduced to one dimension? I refuse to let people think that I am "only" some left-leaning Christian who strives to be part of movements for justice, equity, and love. I'm more complex than that. Online, I also share pictures and stories of my awesome puppies, I am obnoxious about my fandom of the Oakland Athletics Baseball Club, I make fun of myself for the amount of bougie café dining I do, I convey a deep love and commitment to my family, and I am always up for a good GIF battle.

Am I consistent? It's the worst when someone you have only known via Twitter as super insightful and kind turns out to be a grade-A, first-class poopy head in real life. For the most part, I think it's best to maintain consistency between your online and in-person self. When I meet someone and am startled by the difference in tone, content, or general perspective, I am left wondering which one is their real self. Likewise, I find it off-putting and jarring when someone whom I know to be kind in real life turns into an angry troll when they hop online.

At the end of the day, be you. When we are consistent, there are fewer narratives we have to maintain. If we all do this more consistently, we can develop genuinely meaningful relationships that are enhanced by both our online and our in-person interactions and relationships.

Am I as funny as I think? I'm a big believer in the power that satire can have in social movements. Cartoonists, comedians, and writers have been poking and prodding at the powerful for generations. This is a needed part of any movement. But few of us are as witty and wise as we like to think we are. When it comes to the sass that gets bandied about the interweb, our satire is lazy and even hypocritical.

There can only be so many cartoons, memes, and GIFs making fun of politicians, celebrities, and other public figures. To catch my attention, the artist has to have some cutting insight or powerful imagery. Most of my friends are not that talented in this area. Merely expressing opinions or interacting online is an invitation to be trolled; to have people try to seek out and exploit your Achilles' heel; and to receive unsolicited feedback about every fashion, food, or love choice you make. If you apply such filters, your social media and online ecosystem will be built on a spirit of authenticity and fueled by genuine relationships.

A respite from email and the internet can often be re-energizing. So yes, take a break when you need. But our online lives are so important and integrated that developing a healthy and healing posture of being can only be built, nurtured, and embodied when we see one another through the lens of kindness—and act accordingly.

For Reflection:

To what extent are your online and your in-person
lives consistent?

Where do you see the most one-dimensionalizing taking
place online? And where is the most dignity extended?

Try This:

Go back and look through your past weeks or months of
posts and interactions. How many were kind?
What makes them kind?

Kindness and the Impossible

CHOOSING A LIFE of kindness can be overwhelming, and at times that's because kindness does not necessarily make an immediate impact. At other times, trying to be kind is overwhelmingly difficult because of the very situation that has created the need for kindness in the world: Some may bear the weight of a lifetime of institutional and generational racism, homophobia, ableism, misogyny, and so on. Others have lived so long with violence and abuse in relationships that they have accepted them as the way things are. Still others have such physical or mental health issues that the idea of "choosing" cannot be done without significant emotional, spiritual, or medical support.

All of these situations create environments where kindness is the last thing one wants or is able to choose. Rather, these situations have created natural and understandable conditions where distinctly unkind actions are far more accessible choices: self-sabotaging behavior, violent resistance, or other ways of acting that do not honor the humanity of anyone involved.

Now I want to be very clear here: I am not saying that when one experiences pain or violence and acts out behaviors born out of a lifetime of struggle, it is their fault. Nor am I saying that perpetrators or abusers should face no consequences or not be held accountable for their actions. What I *am* saying is that choosing to be kind in the world is not easy.

Choosing a life of kindness is exhausting.

Choosing a life of kindness can also feel impossible, because sometimes it is.

The thing about choosing kindness is that it must become part of our DNA. It is not a tactical switch that we turn on and off at our convenience, but a way of life that we must completely absorb in body, mind, heart, and soul. And while there will always be conflicts and tensions, kindness defaults to actions that value the life and human dignity of all involved. This means that we must make hard choices, for if our commitment lacks depth and is more about convenience, we could spend endless hours and energy doing mental gymnastics to squeeze every response, no matter the impact upon others, into an act of kindness.

Acts of violence toward another human being, no matter how understandable and even justifiable they may be, are not acts of kindness. Self-defense can surely be justified and, one could argue, kind to particular individuals involved. But violence toward another is not an act of kindness. I say the same things in regard to institutional and systemic oppression, violent uprisings, and armed rebellion. That people long oppressed may rise up and find liberation through violent actions I consider not to be grounded in kindness and a sense of human dignity, even though they might be understandable and even justifiable.

Wow, that all got pretty heavy.

I do admit that it is very easy for me to sit here and judge acts of people as kind or not kind. I fully recognize my own privilege and social location and that I can retreat into the comfort of my status and station and look down upon those whose actions may not seem like they are valuing the human dignity of the other.

Again, while some acts are not kind, I do believe they are understandable, and it is this perspective that allows and challenges me to be kind even when it would be justifiable not to be so. I would never encourage violence as a response to unkind acts, but I do understand how one can get to that point. I understand how rage or trauma can get the best of a person and cause someone to lose control and act in a way that is uncharacteristic of them. Anyone who has had a loved one hurt or killed, has been confronted with a life-threatening situation, or has gotten to the point where life's stresses and conditions have transformed into trauma knows that acts of kindness are not always within reach physically, emotionally, or spiritually.

Granted, this is not a natural posture to maintain when we see communities rise up against systems of oppression and counter it with violence, when we see individuals escaping abusive relationships through acts of violence, and when every day there are more people who reach a point at which they find life to be overwhelming. How can we avoid adding to the pain with our judgment, our privilege, or our ambivalence? How can we be part of the healing by exercising our kindness?

When I see these things playing out in the world, I try to commit to kindness and not judgment. How do I do this, you ask? My kindness compels me to think about why these things are happening, to think about the individuals who are part of the events, and to extend a posture of human dignity to all involved. My own kindness forces me to think about the complexities of a person's situation and whether they are there by choice or circumstance. Then I must decide whether that kindness lens is strong enough to see humanity in all those involved, no matter the actions taken or the nature of the situation. Again, this does not mean that perpetrators and offenders should not be held accountable or that victims and the marginalized have in any way brought their suffering upon themselves. It only means that kindness compels me to acknowledge the existence of the inherent humanity of all involved.

Valuing human dignity pushes us to do the hard work that it takes to be part of movements focused on changing institutions and situations that force people to take unkind measures. Committing to the work of kindness compels us to see that the only way these situations will not last forever is if we, and others, value human dignity. And when this human dignity is restored, kindness will be embraced, and healing will be experienced.

Yes, I know that there are many compelling reasons that might make it seem as if this is a foolish stance to take. But as I have said before, to choose our own self-preservation and self-interest over the pain of others is to abdicate the moral voice of our culture and society to those who profit from the oppression and indignity of others. To choose abdication and to devalue the power of kindness in the world is a choice I am not willing to make, and I hope you will not either.

At the end of the day, kindness is not a pill or magic spell that makes it easier to be in the world. Nor should the realization that there will always be pain in the world give us permission to stop trying to be kind. In fact, it should elicit precisely the opposite reaction. Given the many situations that generate destruction, now more than ever kindness is appropriate.

For Reflection:

When was the last time you passed judgment on the "unkind" acts of another person without examining the complexities of why they might have acted in a certain way? How might you participate in a movement to change situations in which people have little choice but to act in unkind ways?

Try This:

Examine a current political uprising that might be perceived as nonpeaceful and parse out the complexities of why this might be happening.

Won't You Choose Kindness?

I n closing, I'll circle back to the Rev. Dr. Fred Rogers, who prompted me to write this book. At the beginning of every episode of *Mister Rogers' Neighborhood*, Fred invited us to be part of something bigger than ourselves. His refrain of "Won't you be my neighbor?" requires us to acknowledge the invitation and to join him in the adventure that it is to be neighbors, to be part of the community of humanity.

Kindness is not a journey for the meek and mild. For those of us who have been steeped in ways of being that are not kind, it takes tremendous energy to purge ourselves of patterns and behaviors that are not kind. Every day we have to choose to commit to live out kindness that day.

Yes, choosing kindness will be exhausting and overwhelming.

Yes, choosing kindness will draw mockery and dismissal.

Yes, choosing kindness will create tension, conflict, and discomfort.

But…

Choosing kindness is an act of courage that challenges a worldview driven by hatred, dishonesty, and dehumanization.

Choosing kindness is about living a life of integrity in which we daily work at resisting the seductiveness of wealth, success, and self-preservation.

Choosing kindness is life-giving. For when we choose to see and respond to the human dignity of any one person, we are all given a little more hope.

And finally, if we do not continue to choose kindness together, can you imagine how much worse the world will become? The least we can do in response to and in gratitude for all those kindness giants who have paved the way is to do the same for the generations to come.

So I hope that you will join me in choosing and defending kindness in all that you do and in forms that are both incredible and incremental. Be a champion for kindness in the institutions in which you work, in your families of birth and choice, amid your faith or social communities, in the hallways of your school, at the café where you are reading this book right now, and wherever there is a chance to extend human dignity to the other.

There is never a bad time to be kind.

It's a matter of choosing to do so.

For Reflection:
What are three ways that you can commit to kindness in the next week?

Think of a community of which you are a part. How might the group make a commitment to kindness?

Try This:
For one week, think back at the end of each day and note moments of kindness, either your own or others'.

ACKNOWLEDGMENTS

There are so many people and creatures in my life who have modeled kindness for me, have affirmed the kindness that they see in me, and challenge me when I am being a jerk.

The humans I call family: Robin, Ev, Abby, and Annie for bringing me joy.

The pups: Vespa, Bernie, and Fawn (RIP 2019) for being excited when we come home.

The rest of my family, who are probably reading this and thinking, "Um, he's listing us after the dogs?"

My friends from the soccer sidelines and parent groups, and colleagues and confidants too abundant to list without leaving someone out.

Organizations and communities that have been part of my kindness arc of learning and practicing kindness: Parents for Public Schools of San Francisco, Rooftop K-8, Drew High School, More Light Presbyterians, Presbyterian Peace Fellowship, Interfaith Movement for Human Integrity, Trinity Presbyterian Church, Mission Bay Community Church, Valley Presbyterian Church in Portola Valley, Broadmoor Presbyterian Church, and First Presbyterian Church of Palo Alto.

The folks at Chalice Press—Brad, Deborah, and Ulrike—for your patience and kindness.

And finally, the de facto patron saint of kindness, Rev. Dr. Mr. Fred Rogers and his partner in life and love, Joanne Rogers! Thank you all.

KEEP IN TOUCH

I WOULD LOVE to stay in touch with you to discuss the book, arrange speaking engagements, or exchange guacamole recipes. Whatever.

Email: bruce@reyes-chow.com

Website: reyes-chow.com

Social media: @breyeschow